20th-Century America

TIME LIFE Student Library

20th-Century America

Time-Life Books   Alexandria, Virginia

Table of Contents

Prelude to the 20th Century

During the 19th century, America underwent tremendous change. The nation itself was only 25 years old in 1801. Sixty years later, just as the nation was becoming established, it faced a civil war that nearly destroyed the Union. Some 180,000 African-American soldiers (*below*) joined the Union ranks to fight for their country and to end 200 years of slavery. When the war was over, Americans were once again united by advances in technology, communication, and transportation.

The population increased, thanks to the arrival of millions of **immigrants,** many of whom settled in the western heartland. Rapid change also brought the need for reforms in schools, women's roles, and the workplace. By the end of the 19th century, the United States had expanded its international role, added 29 new states, and boasted a larger rail system than all of Europe. America was moving and growing—and ready for the challenges of the next century.

Famous **1** FIRSTS

Thomas Edison

Of the more than 1,000 inventions that Thomas Edison patented in his lifetime, none would be more important to the coming century than the first practical electric light, introduced in 1879.

The Wild West

America's frontier had nearly disappeared by 1900. All that remained was Buffalo Bill's Wild West Show featuring such performers as sharp-shooter Annie Oakley.

Public Education

In the 1800s, a system of free schools supported by tax dollars was created in the United States. Only a handful of communities provided education at no cost at first. But by 1900, schools had been established across the land —like this one in Valley Falls, Kansas—and nearly every state required its children to attend.

The Railroads

To lay the lines, railroad crews crossed mountain passes *(left)* and bridged rivers. In 1840, there were 3,000 miles of track in the United States; in 1890, there were nearly 200,000. By 1900, five transcontinental railroad lines crisscrossed the country. The railroads created great wealth for their owners and brought thousands of settlers west, forever changing the lives of Native-American peoples.

Progressive Era — McKinley

During the first **decade** of the 20th century, the United States was becoming a great industrial nation. The first automobile **assembly lines** went into production. Steel and oil industries were booming. **Immigrants** came to the United States in record numbers, boosting the population from 63 million people in 1890 to 93 million people in 1910.

But not all of the changes were positive. Many of the new immigrants were crowded into city slums. They worked long hours at low-paying jobs. And in addition to being unfair to their workers, businesses **bribed** city governments to give them special favors. To stop this corruption, a new political movement called **progressivism** was born. Among its most important leaders was President Theodore "Teddy" Roosevelt.

On September 6, 1901, during his second term in office, President William McKinley was shot in Buffalo, New York. He died eight days later. His attacker was an **anarchist** named Leon Czolgosz, who was tried, convicted, and executed within six weeks.

People — W.E.B. Du Bois

One of the most important African-American leaders of the 20th century was William Edward Burghardt (W.E.B.) Du Bois (1868-1963). He was the first African American to earn a Ph.D. from Harvard University. In 1903 Du Bois wrote *The Souls of Black Folk,* describing what it was like to live in a white-dominated society. In 1909, he helped found the National Association for the Advancement of Colored People (NAACP), an organization that helped African Americans fight for equal rights.

The Panama Canal

Before the Panama Canal was completed in 1914, ships sailing between the Atlantic and Pacific Oceans had to go around the tip of South America. The 82-km (51-mi.)-long canal cut nearly 12,800 km (8,000 mi.) off the trip and shortened travel time between the oceans from two months to less than a day.

Coming to America

During the first decade of the 20th century, more immigrants came to the United States than at any other time in history. In 1907, more than 1.2 million people arrived—the most ever in a single year. Many of these newcomers came from central and eastern Europe, in contrast to earlier immigrants, who had come from western Europe. In the 1920s, the government began to limit the number of people from various nations who could enter the United States.

Roosevelt

When William McKinley died in 1901, Vice President Theodore Roosevelt became president. Popular for his boldness and honesty, he was elected president in his own right in 1904.

William H. Taft

Teddy Roosevelt helped his friend William Howard Taft win the 1908 presidential election. Taft did not support his programs, so Roosevelt ran against him in 1912 (page 18).

Would **You** *Believe?*

The Great San Francisco Earthquake

On April 18, 1906, San Francisco, California, was rocked by the worst earthquake in its history. Scientists estimate the earthquake registered 9.0 on the **Richter scale,** making it one of the strongest quakes ever. Although the earthquake itself was destructive, the three days of fires that followed caused even more damage. About 700 people were killed, and more than half of the city's population lost their homes.

Women on the Move

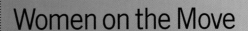

At the beginning of the 20th century, American women demanded their rights in two important areas. In 1909, the International Ladies Garment Workers Union was founded to help women in the clothing industry earn better pay and have shorter workdays. Another goal was suffrage—the right to vote. The woman suffrage movement was started in the 1840s by Elizabeth Cady Stanton, Lucretia Mott, and Susan B. Anthony. By the turn of the century, suffrage marches like the one shown above were a common sight. Women finally gained the vote in 1920 (page 18).

Lively Times

Three of the most popular elements of our modern culture—photography, movies, and radio—were only novelties in 1900. Although photography had been around for more than 50 years, few people were able to take pictures. This changed in 1900, when Kodak introduced the Brownie, the first low-cost, easy-to-use camera.

Italian physicist Guglielmo Marconi had introduced radio, doing most of his work in England and America. At first, Marconi used radio not to transmit voices but to send the dot-and-dash signals of Morse code. The first sounds were not transmitted by radio until 1906.

Moving pictures were invented in the 1890s, but they were not popular until after the turn of the century. Short films were shown in nickelodeons, small theaters named for the price of admission—a nickel. The popularity of nickelodeons created a demand for longer and more-elaborate features.

The First World Series

The first World Series was played in 1903 between the National League champion, the Pittsburgh Pirates, and the American League champion, the Boston Pilgrims (later named the Red Sox). Back then, the best of nine games won the series. The Pilgrims won it, five games to three!

People — Helen Keller

Helen Keller was less than two years old when an illness made her deaf and blind in 1882. Alexander Graham Bell—a teacher of the deaf as well as the inventor of the telephone—introduced Keller to Anne Sullivan, who became her teacher and lifelong friend. With Sullivan as her **interpreter,** Keller graduated from Radcliffe College in 1904. She spent her life as a champion for the disabled.

The First Scout Troops

General Robert Baden-Powell believed that British boys were not as independent or tough as they should be, so he founded the Boy Scouts in 1908. By 1910, Scout troops caught on in the United States, and that same year, Baden-Powell established the Girl Guides in Great Britain. The organization became the Girl Scouts after it came to America in 1912.

What's in a Name?

Teddy Bears

It's hard to imagine, but there were no teddy bears until 1902. That year President Theodore "Teddy" Roosevelt went hunting in Mississippi and refused to shoot a bear cub. The story quickly spread, and a Brooklyn toymaker got the president's permission to name a stuffed bear after him.

Nickelodeons

The motion-picture industry was born when the first movie theaters, called nickelodeons *(left)*, opened in 1905. Placards like the one at top center reminded tobacco-chewing viewers to mind their manners. One of the earliest features was *The Great Train Robbery*, a western that showed a closeup of a gun being fired straight into the camera *(above)*. Viewers who were not used to such movie magic thought real bullets would fly from the screen.

Shutterbugs and Artists

A famous artistic photo of this period is Edward Steichen's tinted shot of the Flatiron Building in New York City *(below)*.

Phone Home!

Although Alexander Graham Bell invented the telephone in 1876, it was not widely used until the first **decade** of the 20th century. The "candle-stick" model shown above was introduced in 1907 and remained popular for decades.

Photography became wildly popular when Kodak introduced the Brownie camera in 1900. For only a dollar, the Brownie came loaded with a six-**exposure** roll of film. When the film was used, it was sent back to Kodak in the camera for processing.

Although the Brownie made photography available to almost everyone, those with real talent created works of art!

The Age of Big Business

In the early 20th century, businesses grew larger and more powerful. In Ohio, John D. Rockefeller's Standard Oil Company dominated the petroleum market. In Pittsburgh, J. P. Morgan's U.S. Steel Company produced most of the nation's steel. And in Detroit, Henry Ford created the first automobile **assembly line** for his Ford Motor Company. Ford's Model T, introduced in 1908, quickly became the world's most popular car.

There were few **regulations** to keep businesses honest or to protect their customers. In 1905, writer Upton Sinclair spent two months working in a meat-packing plant. He **documented** the horrible conditions in his novel *The Jungle (below)*. His work prompted Congress to pass the Pure Food and Drug Act of 1906, which set strict standards for the safe processing of food and medicines.

Children at Work

These young coal miners in Pennsylvania, captured on film by Lewis Hine, faced harsh conditions and long work-hours at an early age. By the turn of the century, more than two million children were working. Not until 1939 did it become illegal to hire children under the age of 14.

"In his own Words"

Upton Sinclair

"There were men who worked in the cooking-rooms, in the midst of steam and sickening odors . . . ; in these rooms the germs of tuberculosis might live for two years. . . . Other men . . . worked in tank rooms full of steam . . . , their peculiar trouble was that they fell into the vats. . . . Sometimes they would be overlooked for days, till all but the bones of them had gone out to the world as Durham's Pure Leaf Lard!"
—Upton Sinclair, *The Jungle*

The Oil Boom

In 1901, drillers struck oil in Spindletop, Texas, triggering an oil boom in the American Southwest. Oil companies sprang up quickly, as this new source of fuel was used to heat homes and run trains.

The giant of the industry was Standard Oil, founded by John D. Rockefeller *(below)* in 1870.

John D. Rockefeller

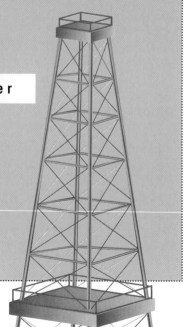

Henry Ford and the Model T

Henry Ford *(right)* was not the first person to build an automobile, but he produced them more quickly and less expensively than anyone else. In 1908, he introduced the Model T *(above)*, nicknamed the Tin Lizzie. About 15 million cars later, America had become a nation of drivers.

The First Harleys

The Harley-Davidson Company was born in a family garage in 1903, when William Harley and brothers Walter, William, and Arthur Davidson built their first motorcycle. The popular bikes were used by the military in World War I, and today Harleys are the only American-made motorcycles.

A Billion-Dollar Company

In 1901, Andrew Carnegie *(page 16)* sold his Carnegie Steel Company to John Pierpont (J. P.) Morgan *(below, right)* for $492 million. Morgan bought out some smaller steel companies to form U.S. Steel, the world's first billion-dollar company. U.S. Steel produced about 7.2 million t (8 million tn.) of steel each year—more than half of the nation's total supply. Morgan was so rich that he was able to bail out the federal government during financial crises in 1893 and 1907.

J. P. Morgan

Discoveries of the Decade

The first **decade** of the century brought discoveries in science and technology that pushed back the frontiers of earth, sky, and space. The skies were conquered by Wilbur and Orville Wright, two bicycle makers from Dayton, Ohio. They built the world's first engine-powered airplane. Robert Peary and Matthew Henson finally reached the North Pole, leaving the South Pole as the last unexplored frontier until 1911. Albert Einstein published his first paper on **relativity**—a theory that shed new light on the workings of the universe.

In medicine, Austrian physician Karl Landsteiner, who spent much of his career in America, discovered three human blood types and developed a blood typing system in 1901. At the same time, his countryman Sigmund Freud established the science of **psychoanalysis,** which opened up a new understanding of how the mind works.

Typhoid Mary

Strange But TRUE!

Mary Mallon, a New York cook, earned a new name for herself in 1907! Doctors discovered that even though she wasn't ill herself, Mary was spreading typhoid fever to the families she served. By the time health authorities finally caught up with her (she reportedly attacked one of them with a carving fork), "Typhoid Mary" had infected 56 people, three of whom died.

Important Imports!

A Thousand Uses!

Today, plastics are everywhere, but the first man-made plastic did not appear until 1907. While working in his New York lab, Belgian-born chemist Leo Baekeland invented a hard rubber substitute he called Bakelite. Known as "the material of a thousand uses," Bakelite soon appeared in many products, from electrical devices to jewelry and handbags.

Sigmund Freud

In 1900, an Austrian doctor named Sigmund Freud changed the way people think about the human mind. His book *The Interpretation of Dreams* explored how the unconscious mind works and what causes mental illnesses. Today he is known as the father of **psychiatry.**

Albert Einstein

German-born physicist Albert Einstein published his theory of relativity in 1905. One of the theory's concepts is that the faster an object travels, the heavier it becomes. Einstein became a U.S. citizen in 1940, and his work shed new light on the workings of our universe.

First in Flight

On December 17, 1903, Orville and Wilbur Wright made history! Orville flew their home-made airplane 36 m (120 ft.) across the beach at Kitty Hawk, North Carolina. It was the first successful powered flight of a heavier-than-air plane. Wilbur died in 1912, but Orville lived until 1948—long enough to see their invention change the world of travel forever.

Halley's Comet

Halley's comet passes earth every 75 years. In 1910, many people feared the comet's dust would poison the earth. The comet proved harmless, and it put on a dazzling show for skywatchers!

Buffalo from the Bronx

By the 20th century, the vast herds of bison that had once roamed the plains were almost extinct. To preserve these animals, New York's Bronx Zoo sent a small herd to Oklahoma in 1907. This and other conservation efforts helped to save the buffalo!

The Pole at Last!

Navy commander Robert Peary had explored the Arctic for 20 years. He tried to reach the North Pole in 1906, but fierce weather forced him back. Two years later, he tried again. With the help of fellow explorer Matthew Henson, Peary and his team finally reached the Pole on April 6, 1909. "The Pole at last!" he wrote in his journal. "My dream and goal of twenty years. Mine at last!" Two years later, Norwegian explorer Roald Amundsen would reach the South Pole—the last un-explored wilderness on earth.

Robert Peary

Matthew Henson

The Changing Face of Business

The 1910s saw some of the best and the worst of the American working world. In fields, factories, and coal mines across the country, workers, including children, toiled for up to 12 hours a day six or seven days a week. While reformers struggled to make life better for low-paid workers, one man changed their lives in another way—by transforming the automobile factory.

Until 1913, each car was made by a skilled worker who built it from start to finish. Then businessman Henry Ford broke down the process of making his Model T cars into its simplest steps. He gave each worker one task—putting together a radiator, for example. The worker would do the same task all day, every day. Since each of the Model T's 4,830 parts was standard, the assembly process was easy.

The **assembly line** was a great success. But as car assembly turned from a skilled job into a tedious one, Ford began having trouble keeping his employees. In 1914 he solved this problem by nearly doubling his workers' salaries, to five dollars a day.

The Triangle Factory Fire

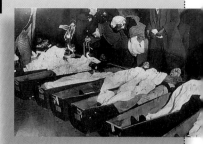

The terrible conditions of New York's garment industry became clear when the Triangle Shirtwaist Factory caught fire in 1911. The flimsy fire escape collapsed, and locked doors—intended to prevent theft—trapped most of the women and girls inside. Ladders on fire trucks could not reach the factory on the eighth floor, and many workers died after leaping out the windows. One hundred forty-six people died in the fire, which led to improved fire codes and new labor laws.

People | Andrew Carnegie

"TO DIE RICH IS TO DIE DISGRACED." JOHN W. GATES—"You will have your wish if you try Chicago wheat."

The sale of his steel company to J. P. Morgan in 1901 made Scottish-born industrialist Andrew Carnegie *(right in illustration at left)* the richest man in the world. He spent the next 18 years giving away $350 million of his fortune. In 1911 he founded the Carnegie Corporation, which still donates money to worthy causes throughout America. "The man who dies rich dies disgraced," Carnegie said.

Labor on the March

Throughout the first half of the 20th century, labor unions made great strides in improving wages and working conditions for their members. In 1912, textile workers in Lawrence, Massachusetts, took to the **picket lines,** faced down armed police *(right),* and got an extra one cent per hour. In 1919 they struck again, demanding that their workweek be reduced to 48 hours. Although this strike failed, later strikes

around the country would not. Thanks to the efforts of labor unions, minimum wages and 40-hour workweeks would eventually become standard for all industries.

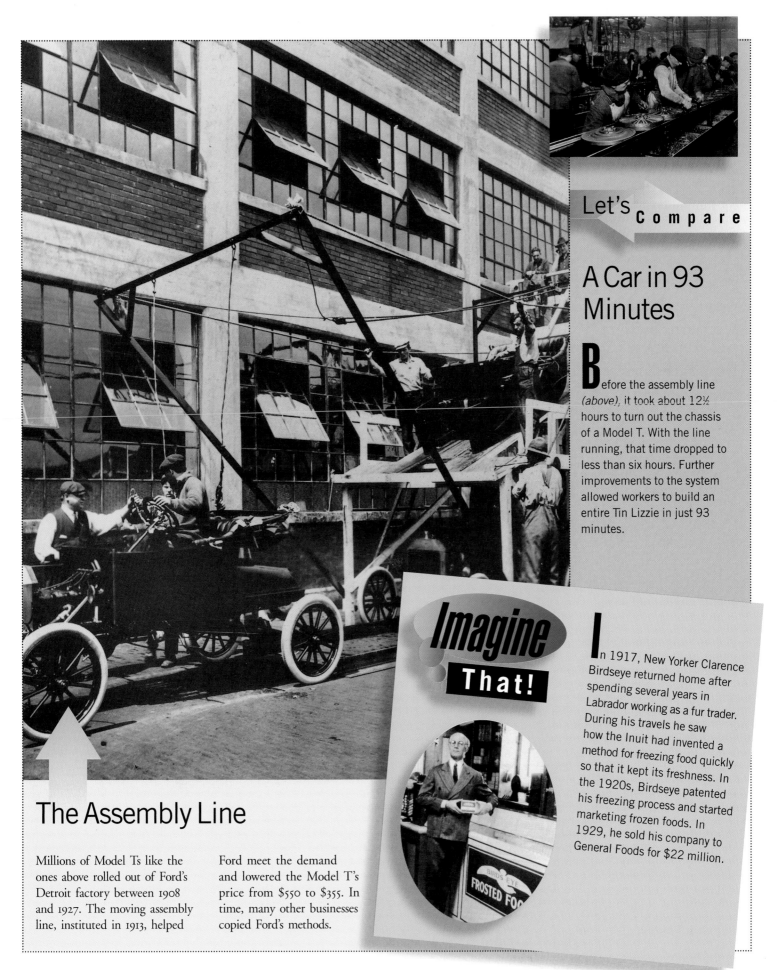

A Car in 93 Minutes

Before the assembly line *(above),* it took about 12½ hours to turn out the chassis of a Model T. With the line running, that time dropped to less than six hours. Further improvements to the system allowed workers to build an entire Tin Lizzie in just 93 minutes.

Imagine That!

In 1917, New Yorker Clarence Birdseye returned home after spending several years in Labrador working as a fur trader. During his travels he saw how the Inuit had invented a method for freezing food quickly so that it kept its freshness. In the 1920s, Birdseye patented his freezing process and started marketing frozen foods. In 1929, he sold his company to General Foods for $22 million.

The Assembly Line

Millions of Model Ts like the ones above rolled out of Ford's Detroit factory between 1908 and 1927. The moving assembly line, instituted in 1913, helped Ford meet the demand and lowered the Model T's price from $550 to $355. In time, many other businesses copied Ford's methods.

The World in Upheaval

In 1914, modern warfare destroyed the old empires of Europe. The conflict had been brewing for years, as European countries, ruled by **aristocrats,** became entangled in secret **alliances** that bound them to come to each other's aid if any one of them was attacked. An **assassin** killed Archduke Franz Ferdinand of the Austro-Hungarian empire (today the countries of Austria and Hungary) in June 1914, and that shot was the spark that ignited the First World War.

Soon Germany declared war on Russia. England, France, and Italy came to Russia's aid (forming the Allied Powers), and Austria-Hungary and Turkey threw their lot in with Germany (forming the Central Powers). Ultimately, countries from all over the world stepped in, with America joining the Allies in 1917. All the Central Powers surrendered by November 1918, but the cost of the war was terrible: Nine million soldiers—50,300 of them American—died in brutal combat and almost 10 million civilians lost their lives.

Famous 1 FIRSTS

Women Get the Vote

The women voting for the first time in New York *(above)* fought a long battle for that right. Although some western states, such as Wyoming, let women vote in state and national elections, it was not until 1920 that the 19th Amendment to the U.S. Constitution allowed all women to vote in national elections.

The Unsinkable *Titanic*

On the night of April 14, 1912, the British ocean liner *Titanic* struck an iceberg on its first voyage. Two hours later, it sank into the North Atlantic. Of the 2,227 passengers and crew, 1,513 died; the supposedly "unsinkable" ship did not carry enough lifeboats. The tragedy led to new safety rules for ships.

TITANIC DISASTER GREAT LOSS OF LIFE EVENING NEWS

What's in a Name?

The Bull Moose Party

When Theodore Roosevelt decided to run for president again in 1912, he couldn't run as a Republican—current president William Howard Taft had won the party's nomination. So Roosevelt became the nominee of the recently formed Progressive Party instead. Soon it was known as the Bull Moose Party, for Roosevelt's boast that he was as "strong as a bull moose." But Roosevelt's entry into the race split the Republican vote. Democrat Woodrow Wilson, the governor of New Jersey, won the election.

America Joins the Fight

Prompted by the famous **recruiting** poster above, thousands of Americans joined the army in World War I. They were posted to battlefields in France *(left)*, where they helped defeat the German forces.

Drawing America into Battle

I n May 1915, a German submarine made headlines *(right)* when it sank the British ocean liner *Lusitania* off the coast of Ireland. Among those lost were 128 Americans, vacationers on their way to Europe. Although some Americans had expressed support for Germany in the early days of the war, that feeling vanished after the *Lusitania* sank. The incident led many in the United States to press for entering World War I on the side of the Allies. President

Woodrow Wilson struggled to keep America neutral, but he found it increasingly difficult. The country finally entered the conflict in April 1917.

People — Eddie Rickenbacker

E ddie Rickenbacker was famous as a racecar driver when he joined the army at the start of World War I. He was assigned to chauffeur General John Pershing, who commanded the American forces, but later he transferred to the Army Air Corps and learned to fly in just 17 days. During the war Rickenbacker shot down 26 German planes to become America's greatest flying ace. Afterward, he bought the Indianapolis Motor Speedway, spent **decades** as the head of Eastern Airlines, and survived two major plane crashes before his death in 1973 at the age of 82.

A World of Entertainment

New frontiers and a modern American spirit brought changes to the world of art and entertainment by 1910. In the early days of motion pictures, most movies were filmed in New Jersey. But by the 1910s moviemakers were looking west, where the weather was better and the locations more varied. The first feature-length western actually shot in the West was made in 1913. The location—a small California town called Hollywood—soon became the home of the movie industry.

When Americans weren't going to the movies, they were enjoying other forms of entertainment. Dancing, for example, had long been seen as **risqué** and immoral. Jazzy popular music and the rise of famous dance teams like Vernon and Irene Castle made dancing more respectable for entertainers and average folks alike.

Important **Imports!**

In 1913 a group of American artists organized a show of European art at New York's 69th Regiment Armory. For many of the 300,000 visitors, it was their first exposure to modern art. Among the most famous pieces on display was Marcel Duchamp's cubist painting *Nude Descending a Staircase (left),* which one critic called "an explosion in a shingle factory."

The Armory Show

Popular Music

Jelly Roll Morton

Ferdinand "Jelly Roll" Morton was a prominent figure in the early history of jazz. The New Orleans-born composer and pianist was among the first to write down and formally arrange his jazz compositions.

Early in the century, many American composers began to break away from European traditions and write music with a fast-paced, distinctly American sound. Irving Berlin, the son of Russian **immigrants,** was one of the most successful.

Irving Berlin

Among Berlin's more than 1,000 songs was his first big hit, "Alexander's Ragtime Band," which he wrote in 1911. The upbeat tune sold more than a million copies of sheet music that year alone.

George M. Cohan

"Over There," written in 1917 by actor, songwriter, and theater producer George M. Cohan, became the anthem of American soldiers going overseas to fight in World War I. By the end of the year, the public had bought more than two million copies of the sheet music.

The Modern Movie

Many of the techniques used in today's movies—such as fade-outs, closeups, and flashbacks—were introduced by film pioneer D. W. Griffith. His breakthrough film was 1915's *Birth of a Nation*, which broke records for its length—three hours; its cost—$110,000; and its ticket price—two dollars. Griffith followed up with another huge production, *Intolerance (below)*, in 1916.

Jim Thorpe

Jim Thorpe, a Native American, was called the world's greatest athlete after winning gold medals for the decathlon and pentathlon in the 1912 Olympics. After the discovery that he had played semipro baseball, which broke Olympic rules, he was stripped of his medals. In 1982, his Olympic records and medals were restored.

Black Studios

Lincoln Motion Pictures was one of a few black-owned companies that made films about black life for **segregated** audiences. Lincoln's *The Trooper of Troop K (below)* featured a heroic black soldier.

The World's Worst Cops

Slapstick comedy brought success to Keystone Studios, founded in 1912 by producer-director Mack Sennett. A former clown, Sennett was keenly aware of what made audiences laugh out loud. He gave it to them in the form of the Keystone Kops, who appeared in a number of Sennett's silent comedies, such as *Keystone Hotel*. In a typical scene, the bumbling Kops would squeeze into their patrol car *(right)*, speed to the scene of a crime, then proceed to make things worse. In addition to creating the Keystone Kops, Sennett's studio also fostered the careers of such future movie stars as Roscoe "Fatty" Arbuckle and Charlie Chaplin.

Lord of the Apes

In 1914, Chicago businessman Edgar Rice Burroughs created an instantly popular folk hero with his novel *Tarzan of the Apes.* He wrote 25 Tarzan books in all.

Science and Medicine

The field of medicine took several important steps forward in the 1910s. In 1912, for example, biochemist Casimir Funk identified the chemicals we now know as vitamins. But at the same time a medical disaster occurred because of something that had been around for centuries: influenza.

Though it was called the Spanish flu, the disease actually began in America in 1918, when soldiers at Fort Riley, Kansas, started to fall ill. Unlike normal strains of flu, the Spanish flu was highly deadly, often killing its victims within two days. It quickly spread around the world, traveling with the troops fighting World War I. A year later it vanished, leaving a worldwide death toll of 20 million people, including some 550,000 Americans. It was one of the worst epidemics in history.

People

George Washington Carver

The brilliance of George Washington Carver (*above, at center*) in chemistry and botany revolutionized agriculture in the South, where years of cotton farming had depleted the soil. His 1914 research report on peanuts and sweet potatoes recommended these crops as replacements for cotton. By the 1940s, peanuts had become the second biggest cash crop in the South.

Rocket Man

The massive rockets that power today's space shuttles grew in large part out of the work done by Robert Hutchings Goddard, a professor of physics at Clark University in Massachusetts. In 1914 he filed the first patents for liquid-fueled, multistage rockets. Skeptics called him Professor Moony, but 12 years later he successfully launched the first of his rockets in Auburn, Massachusetts. It rose only 12.4 m (41 ft.) into the air, but that flight ushered in the space age.

Professor Robert Goddard

Fighting the Flu

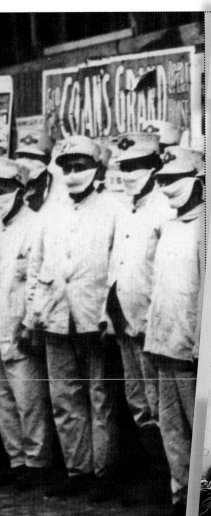

In an effort to slow the spread of the Spanish flu in 1918 and 1919, many people wore face masks outdoors, like the Chicago sanitation workers at left. Children wore small bags of **camphor** around their necks in an attempt to ward off the flu virus, and some cities banned coughing, sneezing, and even shaking hands in public. Despite such efforts, hospitals in America *(below)* and around the world filled up rapidly.

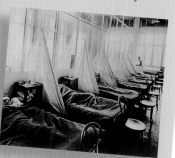

The Plague Returns

Dormant for centuries after killing more than one-fourth of Europe's population in the 14th century, bubonic plague came to America in the 1900s. Roughly 400 San Franciscans died of the plague, which is transmitted to humans from the bites of fleas, who pick it up from infected rats. Once rats were identified as the culprits, big cities moved to eradicate them *(above)* and helped stop the plague.

The Lost City of the Incas

In 1911, a Yale University archaeologist named Hiram Bingham *(far right)* led an expedition to explore the extent of the ancient Inca empire. Braving nearly impassable jungles and mountains high in the Peruvian Andes, the explorer came across the lost city of Machu Picchu *(right)*. Perched between two mountains at an **altitude** of 2,236 m (7,710 ft.), Machu Picchu turned out to be one of the best-preserved ruins of the Inca empire, which stretched from Ecuador to Chile and flourished for centuries before being conquered by the Spanish in 1532. Bingham's excavations revealed that the city contained a temple, a **citadel,** and gardens that were connected by a series of more than 3,000 steps.

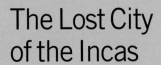

Law and Disorder

Prohibition In—Booze Out

The 1920s were marked by high spirits, wealth, crime, and, in the end, financial disaster. The **decade** began with a great experiment. Members of the **temperance** movement had been arguing for years that liquor was bad for people. So, in 1919 the 18th Amendment was added to the U.S. Constitution; it called for **Prohibition**—a national ban on making and selling alcoholic drinks. However, millions of Americans still wanted to drink, and did, illegally. Gangsters got rich making, importing, and selling alcohol (a practice known as bootlegging).

Bootlegging was profitable, but it couldn't compare with the legal methods for making money. Through most of the decade the economy was booming, and people got rich by buying **stock** in publicly owned companies. All that changed, however, when stock prices fell in the great crash in 1929 *(opposite)*, causing years of economic depression.

Agents of the U.S. Treasury Department—which was charged with enforcing Prohibition—dump barrels of beer into Lake Michigan.

Government agents destroyed all the liquor that they could find, but Americans quickly became very skillful at hiding it.

What's in a Name?

The Untouchables

Treasury agent Eliot Ness *(right, top)* was only 26 when he was given the task of taking down Al Capone *(right, bottom)*, the notorious bootlegging king and mob boss of Chicago. Ness's staff of nine was called the Untouchables for their honesty and refusal to accept **bribes**. Their work resulted in Capone's 1931 conviction and 11-year sentence for income tax evasion.

J. Edgar Hoover and the FBI

Attorney J. Edgar Hoover *(right)* turned the Federal Bureau of Investigation (FBI) into the powerful law-enforcement agency it is today. Hoover was 29 in 1924 when he became director of the bureau. He quickly improved the training of its agents—known as G-men (a nickname for "Government men")—and created the FBI's crime lab. In the 1930s, the FBI and its tough, secretive chief rose to fame as they chased some of the country's most notorious outlaws.

The Crash of '29

Worried businessmen *(right)* gather on New York's Wall Street—the financial center of America—to await news about stock market prices in October 1929. Throughout the 1920s, millions of people bought shares, or stock, in booming companies. On October 24, stock prices started falling, and by October 29 most investors were wiped out. Many people lost their life savings within hours. The crash caused the Great Depression, a time of hardship that lasted until World War II.

Scandal over Teapot Dome

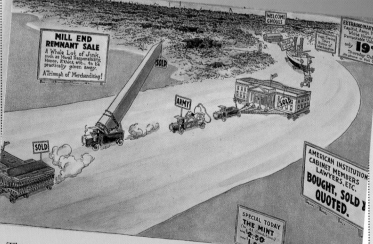

The cartoon above showing government buildings for sale pokes fun at the Teapot Dome **scandal** of the early 1920s. During Warren G. Harding's 1921-1923 presidency, Interior Secretary Albert Fall was convicted of accepting bribes in return for granting private firms drilling rights to federal oil reserves in Teapot Dome, Wyoming.

The Scopes "Monkey" Trial

The 1925 Scopes "monkey" trial pitted prosecutor William Jennings Bryan *(above, right)* against Clarence Darrow *(above, left)*, who defended Tennessee teacher John Scopes against charges that he illegally taught the theory of evolution. Scopes was convicted but later released by the state supreme court.

The Roaring Twenties

At the Movies

The 1920s are often referred to as the Roaring Twenties. A carefree atmosphere had spread across much of the nation. As the economy boomed, many people spent their free time drinking, dancing, and shaking off the restrictive morals of earlier years. The soundtrack for the Roaring Twenties was jazz, a driving, highly individual musical style created by African-American musicians in cities like New Orleans and Chicago. In Harlem, the center of New York City's jazz scene, musicians such as Duke Ellington raised the roof at the Cotton Club and other nightspots.

Harlem also had a crop of brilliant young African-American writers and artists who were finding new ways to celebrate the black experience. Since so many outstanding works were created at the time, the period came to be known as the **Harlem Renaissance.**

Would You Believe?

He's Really Out There

Harold Lloyd became Hollywood's highest-paid comic actor for film escapades like the one above, where he dangled from a clock face in 1923's *Safety Last.* Lloyd performed all of his own stunts.

He's So Sheik

Romantic star Rudolph Valentino made millions of female fans swoon with films like *Son of the Sheik (left).*

Strange But TRUE!

The son of a poor Hungarian family who immigrated to the United States, Ehrich Weiss took the stage name Harry Houdini and became the world's most famous escape artist until his death in 1926. Houdini had a great flair for the dramatic. In one famous stunt *(left)*, he escaped from a locked canister filled with water. In another spectacle, he hung upside down from a 15-m (50-ft.)-high building, shackled and straitjacketed —but freed himself in just minutes.

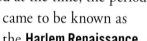

The Little Tramp

Actor Charlie Chaplin, seen at right with his young co-star Jackie Coogan, hit it big with films like *The Kid* (1921) and *The Gold Rush* (1925), in which he played a poor but lovable tramp.

The Jazz Age

Young men and women often danced the night away *(above)* in speakeasies, which sold illegal alcohol. Women showed their modern spirit by wearing short dresses and bobbed hair.

The Hot Five

Cornetist Louis Armstrong *(at piano, above)* was an early innovative and influential jazz musician. His solo **improvisations** helped define jazz style. In 1925, Armstrong led two bands, the Hot Five and the Hot Seven.

Duke Ellington

In 1928, Edward Kennedy "Duke" Ellington and his band headlined at Harlem's famed Cotton Club *(above)*. One of the greatest jazz composers in history, Ellington toured almost continuously until his death in 1974.

Blues Empress

Blessed with a powerful, emotional voice, Bessie Smith *(below)* was the most famous blues singer of the 1920s. Her records "Down Hearted Blues" and "Gulf Coast Blues" sold in the millions.

Langston Hughes

A leading figure of the Harlem Renaissance, writer Langston Hughes (1902-1967) published his first poem at age 18. He went on to write powerful works of poetry, fiction, and drama.

Radio Waves

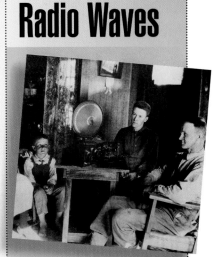

In 1920, Pittsburgh's KDKA began the first regular radio broadcasts in the nation. By the end of the decade there were 618 radio stations nationwide. Between 1922 and 1930 the number of families owning radios also jumped, from 60,000 to 13,750,000.

New Frontiers

The 1920s saw a number of scientific and engineering advances. Some brought people face to face with the immensity of the cosmos. Others simply made household life easier.

In 1927, the world became a smaller place when a 25-year-old aviator named Charles Lindbergh became the first person to fly solo, nonstop, across the Atlantic Ocean. Taking off from Long Island, New York, on May 20, the former airmail pilot landed in a field outside Paris 33½ hours later.

Meanwhile, astronomers found a ninth planet in our own solar system, as well as other galaxies outside our own Milky Way. In fact, they showed that our galaxy was just one of billions in a vast, expanding universe.

Inventing Television

Though it would be decades before televisions found their way into most houses, the first successful TV broadcast took place in 1925. A Scotsman named John Logie Baird (*left, bottom*) sent the image of a puppet from a transmitter in his London lab to a receiver in the next room. Baird's machinery was unwieldy, however. It took two other inventors, Russian-born American Vladimir Zworykin and Utah native Philo T. Farnsworth (*left, top*), to create a practical picture tube similar to the ones used in today's televisions.

Posing with his plane, *Spirit of St. Louis (above)*, Charles Lindbergh shows the can-do attitude that made him an instant hero following his daring transatlantic flight. A crowd of 100,000 met Lindbergh in Paris *(left)* after his landing.

Refrigerators

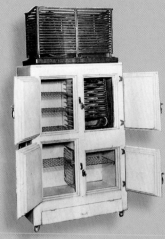

Kitchens everywhere were transformed by the introduction of electric refrigerators in 1923. The new machines quickly replaced the icebox, which—as its name implies— had used a large block of ice to keep food cold.

Scotch Tape

The 3M Company made stickiness a virtue when it began marketing Scotch tape in 1930. Americans used the tape, which was named to remind customers of legendary Scottish thrift, to mend everything from clothing to plaster walls.

The Man behind the Telescope

The Hubble Space Telescope is named after Edwin P. Hubble, who revolutionized astronomy in the 1920s. Working at California's Mount Wilson Observatory, Hubble proved in 1924 that there are countless galaxies outside our own Milky Way, some of them millions of light-years away. A light-year is roughly 9.6 trillion km (6 trillion mi.). Five years later he made an even bigger discovery: All galaxies are rushing away from one another at fantastic speeds. Hubble's discovery supported the big bang theory, which claims that the universe formed in an immense burst of matter and energy.

Welcoming a Ninth Planet

In 1930, while working at Arizona's Lowell Observatory, 24-year-old Clyde Tombaugh discovered the ninth planet in our solar system. The tiny, frigid object, which orbited the sun beyond Neptune, was named Pluto for the Roman god of the underworld. Forty-eight years later, James Christy of the U.S. Naval Observatory discovered that Pluto has a moon. He named it Charon, after the ferryman who carries souls to the underworld.

The Sporting Life

The 1920s have often been referred to as a golden era of American sports. Baseball, football, tennis, golf, and other sports all had legendary players. And although every sport had its heroes, none was bigger than Babe Ruth. Originally a pitcher, he became a right fielder after the Boston Red Sox sold his contract to the New York Yankees in 1919. Ruth led the Yanks to their first World Series win in 1923, making almost as many headlines as a man about town as with his titanic home runs.

Ruth's great stats had a positive effect on the game, which had been rocked by the "Black Sox" **scandal** of 1919, when members of the Chicago White Sox accepted **bribes** to lose the World Series. The happy-go-lucky Babe restored public enthusiasm for the national pastime.

Murderer's Row

First baseman Lou Gehrig and right fielder Babe Ruth *(above, left and right)* were feared as batters in the Yankees lineup, called Murderer's Row. The two took the Yanks to the World Series four times between 1926 and 1932.

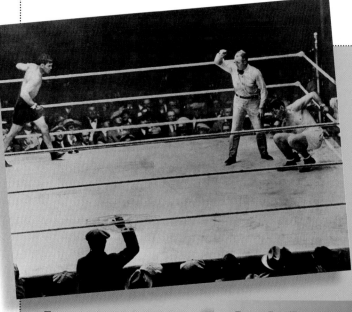

Jack Dempsey

Jack Dempsey, the "Manassa Mauler," was the world heavyweight boxing champion for seven years until his 1926 loss to Gene Tunney. In their rematch in 1927 *(above, with Dempsey at left)*, Dempsey knocked Tunney down in the seventh round, but the referee delayed starting the count. The so-called long count gave Tunney a chance to get up, and he went on to win.

Babe Ruth tees off *(below)* on his record-setting 60th home run in 1927. His record would stand until 1961, when Roger Maris—another Yankee right fielder—belted 61.

Galloping Ghost

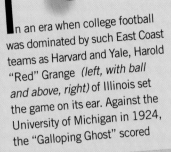

In an era when college football was dominated by such East Coast teams as Harvard and Yale, Harold "Red" Grange *(left, with ball and above, right)* of Illinois set the game on its ear. Against the University of Michigan in 1924, the "Galloping Ghost" scored four touchdowns in the first 12 minutes, adding another later in the game. Grange turned pro in 1925 and became a millionaire playing for the Chicago Bears.

Knute Rockne's Notre Dame

Knute Rockne, a Norwegian immigrant and chemistry teacher, turned Notre Dame into a college football power-house in the 1920s. Between 1919 and 1931 the Fighting Irish had a 105-12-5 record, including undefeated years in 1919, 1920, 1924, 1929, and 1930. The powerful Notre Dame backfield of the early 1920s *(right)* was nicknamed The Four Horsemen, after the biblical Four Horsemen of the Apocalypse, who left death and devastation behind them.

On the Court

Tennis star Bill Tilden *(below)* won seven U.S. singles titles between 1920 and 1929, while Helen Wills *(right)* matched that feat between 1923 and 1931. Wills's seriousness on the court earned her the nickname Little Miss Poker Face.

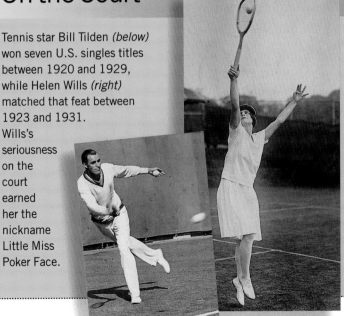

Links Master

Georgia lawyer and amateur golfer Bobby Jones made history when he became the first to win golf's grand slam—all four major tournaments—in 1930.

Hard Times

What's in a Name?

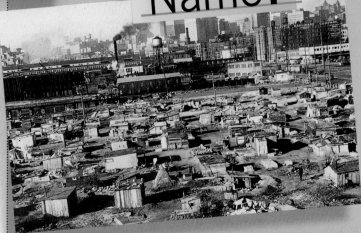

Hoovervilles

When **stock** prices crashed in 1929 *(page 25)*, banks failed, businesses closed, people lost their jobs, and international trade suffered. The era that followed became known as the Great Depression—the worst economic collapse in American history. When parents lost their jobs, children sometimes went to live with other family members. To help their families survive, three million children between the ages of seven and 17 left school and went to work.

Record heat and drought in the Midwest caused crops to fail, and dry winds created massive dust storms that carried away the rich topsoil. A huge area in the Midwest became known as the Dust Bowl. As farms failed, 750,000 farmers went west with their families to find work in California, Oregon, and Washington—one of the largest **migrations** in the nation's history!

As people lost their jobs and their homes, they built shacks of cardboard and scrap lumber, similar to this group on the edge of Seattle in 1933.

People called these cardboard villages Hoovervilles, named for President Herbert Hoover, who was blamed for causing the economic crisis.

Black Blizzards

An Oklahoma farmer and his sons struggle in a fierce dust storm in 1936. The churning, suffocating storms—called black blizzards—had winds up to 150 km/h (90 mph).

The Bonus Army

About 20,000 jobless World War I veterans marched on Washington, D.C., in 1932. They demanded early payment of a promised bonus for wartime service. Federal troops finally chased them from their camps on the Capitol lawn.

I Was There!

"**T**hese storms were like rolling black smoke. We had to keep the lights on all day. We went to school with headlights on and with dust masks on. I saw a woman who thought the world was coming to an end."

—a Texas schoolboy

WORLD'S HIGHEST STANDARD OF LIVING

There's no way like the American Way

American Dream on Hold

In Louisville, Kentucky, hungry flood victims wait for food in a 1937 **bread line.** The billboard in the background shows a happy, well-fed family—a false image of American life at the time. President Franklin Roosevelt declared that one-third of the nation was "ill-housed, ill-clad, ill-nourished." Charities that served bread and soup to the poor were stretched to the limit. President Roosevelt asked the government to provide more help for those in need.

Hindenburg Disaster

In 1937, the world's largest airship exploded in a tragic accident over New Jersey. As the *Hindenburg* was docking, its hydrogen ignited. Thirty-six people were killed, but 62 others were able to escape with help from a landing crew on the scene. The gas-filled **zeppelins** would never again be used to carry paying passengers.

Let's Compare

Unemployment Rates

As the Depression dragged on, the number of people without jobs grew from four million in 1930, to 12 million in 1932. By 1933, **unemployment** reached an all-time high of 24.9 percent, or about 15 million people. Some wages were as low as five cents an hour. Production needed for World War II finally created enough jobs to lower unemployment rates again.

Year	Rate
1929	3.2%
1933	24.9%
1944	1.2%

Nature on the Rampage

The Ohio River swallowed up Louisville, Kentucky, in 1937 and created the greatest emergency for the Red Cross since World War I. Nearly a million people were **evacuated.** Unfortunately, local governments and private charities had run out of money for flood relief.

During the 1930s, the nation suffered the worst series of natural disasters in its history. As floods swept away nine million homes in the East, families in the Midwest faced a severe drought. The Roosevelt administration called for government assistance for the victims (page 34).

New Deal for America

I n 1932, newly elected president Franklin Delano Roosevelt (FDR) promised all Americans a New Deal. He called for "action, and action now" to help the nation recover from the Great Depression. The first hundred days of his presidency were the most productive in U.S. history. An emergency session of Congress passed 15 historic bills for social legislation and financial reforms. The Emergency Banking Act restored confidence in banks after widespread failures in 1929. People were put back to work building public roads, dams, bridges, schools, power plants, and hospitals. New laws banned child labor and limited the number of hours in a workweek. Although FDR was crippled by **polio** *(page 55)* and was unable to walk without help, he was the first and only president to be elected to four consecutive terms in office.

First Lady "Eleanor Everywhere"

I n 1939, Eleanor Roosevelt presents a medal to opera singer Marian Anderson from the National Association for the Advancement of Colored People (NAACP). When the Daughters of the American Revolution barred Miss Anderson from performing in Constitution Hall because of her race, Mrs. Roosevelt resigned from the group. A champion for equal rights for women and African Americans, the first lady traveled the nation as the "eyes and ears" for her wheelchair-bound husband, earning the nickname Eleanor Everywhere.

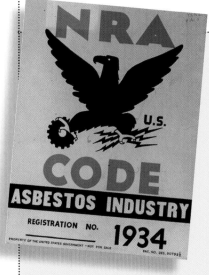

The NRA Eagle

I n 1933, two million people gathered in New York City to watch a parade of 250,000 flag-waving supporters *(below)* of the National Recovery Administration (NRA). Businesses displayed the NRA eagle *(left)* to show people they were part of a national effort aimed at controlling prices and wages and stimulating growth.

Alphabet Soup

Franklin Roosevelt's New Deal created agencies and services that put millions of people back to work. The programs, known by their initials, were nicknamed alphabet soup.

CCC	Civilian Conservation Corps
WPA	Works Progress Administration
SEC	Securities and Exchange Commission
FHA	Federal Housing Administration
TVA	Tennessee Valley Authority

"The only thing we have to fear is fear itself." —Franklin D. Roosevelt

During his first campaign, in 1932, Franklin Roosevelt *(far right)* promised to help the nation's workers. He scored a landslide victory over Herbert Hoover, winning by seven million popular votes.

New Deal for American Indians

A monthly check to you—

FOR THE REST OF YOUR LIFE • • BEGINNING WHEN YOU ARE 65

GET YOUR SOCIAL SECURITY ACCOUNT NUMBER *promptly*

APPLICATIONS ARE BEING DISTRIBUTED AT ALL WORK PLACES

WHO IS ELIGIBLE — EVERYBODY WORKING UNDER CIVIL A FOR EXCEPTIONS, SUCH AS AGRICULTURAL COVERAGE WORK • APPLICATIONS FOR SOCIAL SECUR

INFO

Hoover Dam

Rising 220 m (726 ft.) above the Colorado River, the Hoover Dam *(right)* holds 378.54 trillion l (100 trillion gal.) of water. It was built by the WPA to control floods and provide electricity. The WPA hired artist William Gropper to paint a mural *(above)* of the dam's construction.

In 1934, Commissioner of Indian Affairs John Collier welcomed Native-American leaders to Washington, D.C., when the Indian Reorganization Act restored their lands and granted them self-government.

Famous 1 FIRSTS

The Social Security Act was signed into law in 1935 to protect families from lost income resulting from a death, disability, or **unemployment.** The poster shown above encourages Americans to apply for a Social Security number.

High Times

A s Americans struggled through the Depression in the 1930s, they found some ways to have fun and forget their worries—at least for a while. National radio networks began to broadcast programs coast to coast, allowing anyone to hear the latest news, music, popular comedy, drama, and variety shows. In the world of sports, baseball was the national pastime, Joe Louis became the heavyweight champ, and Jesse Owens dominated the 1936 Olympic Games in Berlin, Germany.

Hollywood helped people relax by producing big-screen movie musicals and dramas. Color films like *Gone with the Wind* and *The Wizard of Oz* brought fantasy to life as never before. New amusements such as pinball games and comic books also caught on. The problems of the day remained, but entertainment made them easier to face.

Jesse Owens

In 1936, track star Jesse Owens streaked for gold in the Olympic Games held in Berlin, Germany. When this talented black athlete won four gold medals, German dictator Adolf Hitler was stunned. Owens had punched holes in Hitler's theory of **Aryan** superiority. He received a hero's welcome when he returned home.

Would **You** *Believe?*

The Night Mars Attacked

F amilies fled their homes. Traffic backed up for miles. Phone lines were jammed. On the night of October 30, 1938, a radio broadcast of *The War of the Worlds,* a classic science-fiction tale by H. G. Wells *(left, top),* had many listeners sure that real Martians had landed. The next morning, Orson Welles, the program's young producer *(left, bottom),* apologized for his scary Halloween story. The power of radio could not be ignored!

A League Apart

D uring the 1920s, '30s, and '40s, some of the nation's best baseball players were not in the major leagues. Because of **segregation,** African-American players had their own leagues. Teams such as the Kansas City Monarchs, Homestead Grays, and Pittsburgh Crawfords *(above)* drove across the nation, playing an afternoon game in one town and moving on to the next before nightfall. Fans flocked to see stars such as pitching ace Leroy "Satchel" Paige, slugger Josh Gibson, and base runner James "Cool Papa" Bell. The Negro leagues would thrive until 1947, when Jackie Robinson signed with the Brooklyn Dodgers and became the first black player in the major leagues.

On the Silver Screen

Escape to Oz

In 1939, moviegoers were off to see the wizard—the wonderful *Wizard of Oz.* Based on a book by L. Frank Baum, the movie took viewers on a magical journey "somewhere over the rainbow." Singer and actress Judy Garland *(right)* played the heroine, Dorothy.

Monstermania

Frankenstein. Dracula. The Mummy. These movie monsters were the first of their kind. When horror movies appeared in the 1930s, fans screamed for more. Viewers agreed that a good scare was good fun!

Pinball Daze

When kids had a few cents to spare, they would go to the **penny arcade.** In 1930, a new game called Baffle Ball challenged players to shoot steel balls into scoring rings formed by small pins. More than 50,000 machines were sold, launching a pinball craze! Jigsaw, the game at left, came out in 1932.

Board Games

New board games have long provided fun for the whole family. In 1935, the MONOPOLY® game was introduced and became an instant hit. Its theme was right for the times, since each player could spend bundles of imaginary cash on property. It is still an American favorite.

The Biggest Little Star

On gray days, a movie starring Shirley Temple *(right)* brought sunshine. Singing and tap-dancing her way through a dozen movies during the **decade,** this little girl was one of Hollywood's biggest stars. Her famous dimples and curls graced dolls *(far right),* soap, books, and even underwear!

Man of Steel

In 1938, Action Comics introduced Superman, a visitor from the planet Krypton who uses his superpowers to fight evil and rescue people in danger. Disguised as newspaper reporter Clark Kent, Superman is able to find out about trouble quickly. The popular comic book hero also became a hit on radio and TV and in the movies *(page 82).*

Higher, Faster, Farther

Defying the gloomy mood of the Great Depression, American dreamers, adventurers, and engineers pushed innovation to new heights. Early in the **decade,** the Empire State Building rose above the New York skyline, becoming the tallest building on earth. On the other side of the country, the Golden Gate Bridge sparkled in the sunlight. The new 1,400-m (4,200-ft.) suspension bridge was the longest in the world.

Aviation was still a new frontier, and new flying machines, like the helicopter, were just taking off. Daring fliers, such as Amelia Earhart and Wiley Post, broke air records for speed, distance, and **altitude.** And the amazing inventions of the 1939 World's Fair in New York gave Americans hope for a brighter future.

The 1939 World's Fair

As he welcomed exhibitors and visitors from more than 60 nations, Franklin Roosevelt opened the 1939 New York World's Fair with these words: "All those who come will find that the eyes of the United States are fixed on the future." Indeed, the theme of the fair, "Building the World of Tomorrow," gave visitors a dazzling glimpse of the coming age. They marveled at such novelties as refrigerators with automatic icemakers, nylon stockings, model cities with 14-lane highways, and a radio with pictures (called television)!

People — Amelia Earhart

Determined and fearless, Amelia Earhart loved to fly! Ignoring the limits placed on women, she set record after record, becoming a symbol of America's can-do spirit. On June 1, 1937, she set off with a navigator to become the first woman pilot to fly around the world. Radio contact with Earhart was lost over the Pacific, and her plane vanished without a trace. Some researchers think they've found a crash site, but Earhart's disappearance remains a great mystery.

The Golden Gate Bridge

After

Before

Spanning the San Francisco Bay, the Golden Gate Bridge took four years to build. When it opened in 1937, the 1,400-m (4,200-ft.) suspension bridge was the world's longest—and an instant landmark.

The First Helicopter

Leonardo da Vinci designed a helicopter in the 16th century, but it didn't get off the ground until the 1930s. Using rotors instead of fixed wings, helicopters can move straight up and down, hover in one place, and fly in any direction. German engineer Heinrich Focke built the first twin-rotor version in 1936. But Russian-born Igor Sikorsky flew the first practical helicopter in Bridgeport, Connecticut, in 1939. Most helicopters in use today are based on his model.

How Tall?

More than 440 m (1,453 ft.) high, New York's Empire State Building towered over every other building in the world. When it opened on May 1, 1931, the art deco skyscraper featured 102 floors, 6,500 windows, and a mooring mast for **dirigibles.**

Pioneer Spaceman!

With his neat mustache and eye patch, Wiley Post was a dashing figure. By 1934, he had made two record-setting flights around the world. His next adventure sent him almost to the **stratosphere.** Wearing a pressurized suit *(right)* that made him look more like a deep-sea diver than an astronaut, Post flew to a height of nearly 15.2 km (9.5 mi.), setting a new altitude record.

Wiley Post's 1934 Altitude Record: 15.2 km (9.5 mi.) above the Earth

How High?

Stratosphere
16-48 km (10-30 mi.) above Earth

Troposphere
16 km (10 mi.) above Earth

Earth

WWII: War in the Pacific

In December 1941, most Americans were not worried about Japan. The Asian country was far from the European war that filled most people's minds. So it came as a horrible shock when Japanese bombers attacked American ships at Pearl Harbor in Hawaii. Unexpectedly, America was at war—in the Pacific.

Millions volunteered or were drafted into service. Patriotism soared, along with tearful good-byes. Americans fought the war united in their love of country, but in a few instances that love was severely tested. Even as wartime **hysteria** led the government to imprison Japanese Americans in **relocation camps,** thousands of their sons served in the military, fighting bravely with their fellow Americans in the Second World War.

Good-Bye, Dad

Soldiers said fond farewells *(above)* around the clock at train and bus stations as some 16 million men entered the U.S. military during World War II. Families could only hope for the safe return of husbands, fathers, sons, and brothers.

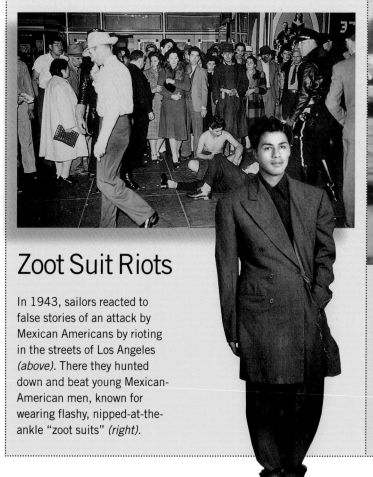

Zoot Suit Riots

In 1943, sailors reacted to false stories of an attack by Mexican Americans by rioting in the streets of Los Angeles *(above)*. There they hunted down and beat young Mexican-American men, known for wearing flashy, nipped-at-the-ankle "zoot suits" *(right)*.

Day of Infamy

It came without warning. On the morning of December 7, 1941, 183 Japanese planes appeared over Pearl Harbor, an American naval base in Hawaii. Japan's deadly bombing and strafing runs destroyed 18 warships, including the USS *Shaw (above),* and 188 planes, killing 2,433 soldiers. The next day, the United States declared war on Japan, officially entering World War II.

Citizen Prisoners

Strong anti-Japanese feelings led to the **internment** of all people with Japanese ancestry living on the West Coast. Over half of the **Nisei** were American born. Forced into government relocation camps *(right, top)*, they became prisoners in their own land.

Daniel Inouye

Even as the relocation camps filled, more than 25,000 Japanese Americans were serving in the U.S. armed forces. Among them was Daniel Inouye *(right)*, a future U.S. senator from Hawaii.

Raise the Flag

The small island of Iwo Jima was the site of one of the bloodiest battles in the Pacific. U.S. troops landed there February 19, 1945, hoping to set up a landing site for American bombers. Marines raised the American flag atop the island's Mount Suribachi four days later *(left)*, but the fighting lasted almost a month, killing more than 6,000 Americans.

Would You Believe?

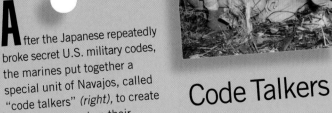

Code Talkers

After the Japanese repeatedly broke secret U.S. military codes, the marines put together a special unit of Navajos, called "code talkers" *(right)*, to create new codes based on their native language. This Navajo code was never broken.

WWII: War in Europe

By the time the United States declared war on Japan, the European conflict was already in high gear. Germany had invaded Poland in 1939, occupied France in 1940, and marched into Russia in 1941. Four days after Pearl Harbor, the United States entered the European war as well, joining Great Britain and Russia as one of the Allied nations against the Axis forces of Germany, Italy, and Japan.

Much of World War II was fought in the air. New planes could fly farther and faster and carry more ammunition. Allied bombers destroyed key German locations, while the German **blitzkrieg** rained terror on French and British civilians. American factories worked around the clock to make the weapons needed to defeat the Axis armies.

D-Day

On the morning of D-Day, June 6, 1944, Allied soldiers launched the greatest **amphibious** assault in history. An **armada** of some 5,000 vessels converged on Normandy, France. More than 150,000 Allied soldiers hit the beaches under heavy gunfire. The surprise attack turned the tide of the war.

War on the Ground

The Air War

Long before they sent in the infantry, the Allies fought Germany from the air. British planes preferred to strike under cover of night, whereas American bombers like this B-17 *(above)* often flew raids in broad day-light, staying at high **altitudes**. The air war was fought at great risk: Germany shot down 18,500 U.S. planes, killing 64,000 airmen. But by 1944, strategic air attacks had slowed down the German war machine.

Technology had improved battle-ships and warplanes, but common foot soldiers, such as these firing a powerful howitzer cannon *(above),* were the army's main weapon. Most were equipped with only a rifle, ammunition, and their own courage. From the initials for "Government Issue" on their equipment, U.S. soldiers gave themselves the nickname GI.

Joining the War on the Home Front

Famous **1** FIRSTS

WACs, WAVES, and WASPs

The army's Women's Army Corps (WAC), the navy's Women Accepted for Volunteer Emergency Service (WAVES) and the air force's Women's Air Force Service Pilots (WASP) each served vital noncombat roles. About 200,000 women joined these **auxiliary** units, doing such jobs as flying planes from factories to bases and teaching gunnery.

Working Women

The figure of a strong, capable woman *(far left)* shines from a poster urging women to take on traditionally male jobs. When men went to war, women across the United States, such as these workers in an aviation plant *(left),* took over many of their jobs. Though paid less than men, women gained a new confidence and sense of fellowship by excelling at these normally male-only jobs.

People

Adolf Hitler

Forceful. Charismatic. Evil. Insane. These words are often used to describe Adolf Hitler *(above),* Germany's leader during World War II. Born in 1889, Hitler helped form the Nazi Party in 1919. He put forth an **ideology** that preached racial superiority, **nationalism,** and scorn for democracy. Elected to head the German government in 1933, Hitler built up Germany's military, eventually using it to invade his neighbors. In 1945, with Allied bombs landing near his door, Hitler committed suicide.

Kids Contribute

Children helped with the war effort by gathering rubber and aluminum scrap for recycling *(right).* The government relaxed child labor laws during the war years, opening defense industry jobs to teenagers *(far right).* Teens were perfect for some jobs: They could work in spaces too small for adults.

WWII: The Aftermath

Within months of the invasion at Normandy, the Allies had retaken much of Europe. The final push took almost a year, but on May 7, 1945, Germany surrendered. The joy that erupted all over the world turned to horror when soldiers opened up Hitler's **concentration camps.**

Meanwhile the focus shifted to Japan. America had won several key battles in the Pacific, but the victories had cost many lives. President Truman decided to use the newly developed atomic bomb to force Japan to surrender. On August 6, 1945, an atomic bomb **vaporized** the heart of Hiroshima. Three days later, another fell on Nagasaki. On September 2, 1945, Japan formally surrendered. World War II was over.

Fast FACTS

Some 35 million lives were lost during World War II. Deaths among Allied and Axis countries included:

Russia	18 million
Germany	4.2 million
Japan	1.97 million
Great Britain	466,000
Italy	395,000
United States	298,000

The effort was costly in dollars, as well. By the war's end, the United States had spent $82 billion.

People — Audie Murphy

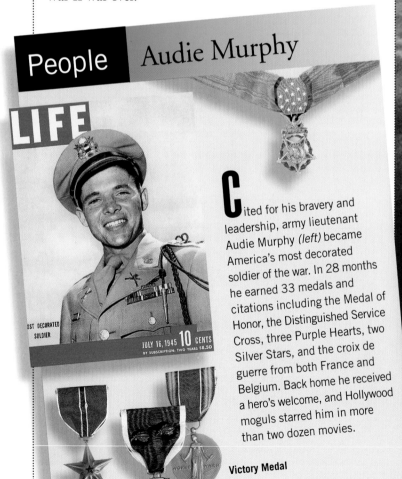

LIFE

MOST DECORATED SOLDIER

JULY 16, 1945 · 10 CENTS
BY SUBSCRIPTION; TWO YEARS $8.50

Cited for his bravery and leadership, army lieutenant Audie Murphy (left) became America's most decorated soldier of the war. In 28 months he earned 33 medals and citations including the Medal of Honor, the Distinguished Service Cross, three Purple Hearts, two Silver Stars, and the croix de guerre from both France and Belgium. Back home he received a hero's welcome, and Hollywood moguls starred him in more than two dozen movies.

Victory Medal

Bronze Star

Purple Heart

Mushroom clouds above Nagasaki were the sign of a powerful new weapon. The two atomic blasts in Japan killed 150,000 people.

The Liberation of Paris

When American troops marched into Paris in August 1944, driving out the Germans, Parisians ran into the streets in a frenzied celebration. For four years they had endured Nazi rule, with food shortages and electricity that flowed only one hour a day. One American captain described the Paris crowds as a "physical wave of human emotion." Incensed, Hitler ordered Paris destroyed, but German officers ignored his command.

Hitler's Death Camps

As Allied troops took control of German territory, they freed prisoners of war *(right)* and inmates of concentration camps. The soldiers were greeted by starving Jewish prisoners and stacks of dead bodies. Hitler hated the Jewish people, calling them "racially inferior" and blaming them for many of Germany's problems. As part of his Final Solution, he set out to kill them all in concentration camps. About six million Jews and five million other "undesirables" died there, many shot, gassed, starved, or worked to death.

Chart

The Nazis committed **genocide** on a scale that the world had never seen before. Among their victims were:

Eastern European Slavs	10,547,000
Jews	5,291,000
Roma (Gypsies)	258,000
Homosexuals	220,000

A Bomb Called Fat Man

The scientists who developed the atomic bomb that destroyed Nagasaki referred to it as Fat Man. It weighed 10,000 pounds. Its explosive power, which came from splitting plutonium atoms, equaled 20,000 tons of **TNT.**

They Called It V-J Day

In August 1945, a nationwide party began. Three years, eight months, and six days after the United States entered World War II, the fighting was over. Immediately after President Truman released the news that Japan had surrendered, big-city streets and small-town squares were flooded with people whooping it up in instant celebration.

Strangers kissed, hugged, and cried in one another's arms. In San Francisco, air-raid sirens wailed. In Washington, D.C., military police were called to stop a gleeful march onto the White House grounds. Two million ecstatic people jammed Times Square in New York *(left).* One GI remembered it as the "kissingest day in history."

Coming Home to the Good Life

As World War II ended, millions of servicemen and -women returned to an America waiting to bust loose after years of sacrifice and anxiety. Now a major player on the world stage, the country was ready to flex its muscle at home. The new spirit was displayed in loud music; fast cars; and new, improved gadgets for the home. Now, more than ever, that home was a single-family house in the suburbs with its own yard, driveway, and two-car garage.

Returning soldiers got a boost from the GI Bill, enacted in 1944. This government program offered benefits such as no-interest home loans and college tuition. Great job opportunities in the surging economy fostered an optimistic view of the country's future.

GI Joe Goes to College

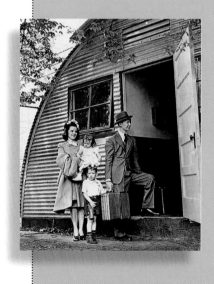

Willard Pedrick, a former marine lieutenant, moves with his family into a **Quonset hut** *(left)* on the campus of Northwestern University after the war. The metal house and others like it were a hasty response to the huge numbers of new students entering college under the GI Bill. The bill, which provided four years of college tuition, included money for housing for families of service-men and -women returning from the war. About 7.8 million veterans took advantage of the offer to pay for an education that might otherwise have been much too expensive.

Run on Nylon

In 1945, the first sale of nylon stockings after the war excited some customers so much that they put the hosiery on in the street. The fabric had been restricted to military use during the war.

In the Modern Home

Women with postwar dollars to spend became the targets of companies selling new housework helpers. The modern 1940s kitchen *(below)* might have an electric mixer; automatic dishwasher; and larger, fancier refrigerator and washing machine.

Daddy's Home

Soldiers returning at the end of the war sometimes had to get reacquainted with children they barely knew. Within a year after V-J Day, most servicemen were civilians once more.

The Lindy Hop

Dancers of the '40s literally took to the air *(below)* as they danced the lindy hop. The lindy hop's lightning-fast, acrobatic moves were a perfect match for the new, urgent rhythms of swing and bebop.

Jukebox as Art

Led by the Wurlitzer Company, which made some of the most beautiful machines of the era *(above),* colorful jukeboxes played popular tunes at the drop of a coin.

Teen Scene

Enjoying their new prosperity, young people *(left)* crowded into malt shops, record stores, and movie theaters looking for ways to spend their money and **leisure** time.

Strange But TRUE!

Flying Saucers

FATE
VOLUME 1   NUMBER 1

THE TRUTH ABOUT
THE FLYING SAUCERS
By KENNETH ARNOLD

MARK TWAIN AND
HALLEY'S COMET
By HAROLD M. SHERMAN

INVISIBLE BEINGS
WALK THE EARTH
By R. L. CRESCENZI

TWENTY MILLION
MANIACS
By G. H. IRWIN

Many Other Startling
Articles And Features

The FLYING DISKS

In June 1947, a pilot flying his private plane over Mount Rainier, Washington, reported seeing a fast-moving, disk-shaped craft. A month later, a sheep rancher near Roswell, New Mexico, found thin, metallic pieces of what newspapers reported as a "flying disk." Hundreds of saucer sightings followed around the country. Rumors circulated that the air force was hiding bodies of alien crash victims. Despite attempts by various sources to discredit sightings, UFO mania had landed in America.

What's NEW in the '40s

Silly Putty
THE REAL SOLID LIQUID

It started out as a substitute for rubber. But when that didn't work out, the bouncing goo ended up as Silly Putty, known as "the toy with one movable part."

It's Slinky

One day in 1943, an engineer saw a spring fall from a shelf and start to "walk." Two years later his simple Slinky was a toy sensation, a success that stretches to this day.

American All-Stars

Then & NOW!

It was a time for inspiration and heroics, and the personalities and entertainment of the age didn't disappoint. Sports stars of the day included baseball heroes "Joltin' Joe" DiMaggio and Jackie Robinson. The fleet-footed athleticism of Sugar Ray Robinson and the awesome punching power of Joe Louis made them legendary kings of the ring.

On the silver screen, Humphrey Bogart brawled; Gene Kelly danced; Frank Sinatra sang; and actresses such as Rita Hayworth, Ava Gardner, and Lauren Bacall set the standard for glamour. In the late 1940s, TV brought celebrities, including comedian Milton Berle and a puppet named Howdy Doody, into the home. And in several newspapers, the "Peanuts" gang quickly became comic strip superstars.

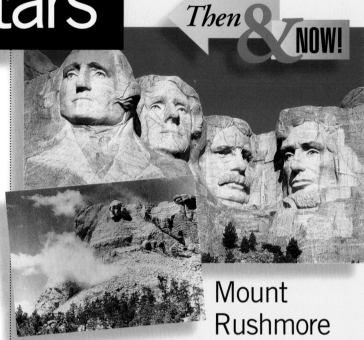

Mount Rushmore

Sculptor Gutzon Borglum began with George Washington's head (above, left), as tall as a six-story building. Fourteen years later, in October 1941, the monument to Presidents Washington, Jefferson, Theodore Roosevelt, and Lincoln on South Dakota's Mount Rushmore (top) was completed.

Good Ol' Charlie Brown

What's NEW in the '40s

Comic strip character Charlie Brown (below) first appeared in papers in 1950. His creator, Charles Schulz, once noted, "Happiness does not create humor." Indeed, his lovable losers Charlie Brown, Lucy, Linus, and Snoopy were usually plagued by worries.

GOOD OL' CHARLIE BROWN.....YES, SIR!

RE COMES LIE BROWN!

Dewey Wins?

Vice President Harry Truman became president after the death of President Roosevelt in April 1945. For a while he was so unpopular that the Chicago Daily Tribune (right) mistakenly announced his loss in the 1948 presidential election.

The Jefferson Memorial

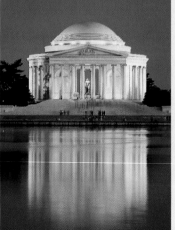

A bronze sculpture of Thomas Jefferson looks out over the Tidal Basin from the Jefferson Memorial (left) in Washington, D.C. The memorial was dedicated in 1943, on the 200th anniversary of Jefferson's birth. The round marble building reflects Jefferson's love of classical architecture.

Sluggers

DiMaggio

"Joltin' Joe" DiMaggio thrilled Yankees fans—and the rest of America—with his 56-game hitting streak in 1941.

Robinson

Jackie Robinson, the first African American to play in the majors, had stellar skills that made him Rookie of the Year in 1947.

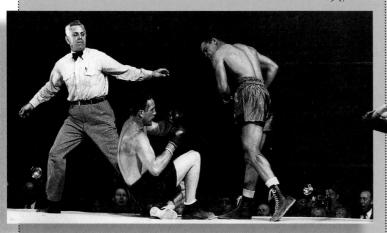

Louis

Heavyweight champ from 1937 until 1949, Joe Louis had 26 wins and 22 knockouts.

Music

The Voice

In 1941, as a performer with the Tommy Dorsey Orchestra, Frank Sinatra (right, top) was voted the most popular singer in the country. He soon went solo and revolutionized pop singing with a unique style that left his female fans (right) swooning and screaming for more.

The Bandleader

Throughout the 1940s, the Big Band sound was king, and one of the most popular orchestras was led by Glenn Miller (left). The bespectacled trombone player led his band in a string of hits including "Chattanooga Choo-Choo" and "In the Mood."

Country King

In 1949, country singer Hank Williams hit it big with "Lovesick Blues." He also wrote and sang the classics "Your Cheatin' Heart" and "Hey Good Lookin'."

The Trio

The sparkling harmonies of the Andrews Sisters (left) lifted spirits during World War II. The sisters traveled extensively, entertaining the troops and raising money for war bonds.

A Decade for Big Ideas

How Big?

Stimulated first by the war and then by a booming economy, the 1940s witnessed huge advances in science and technology. The **decade** brought inventions, from the tiny transistor to the massive atomic bomb, that changed the world. Also making news were breakthroughs in medicine, including the development of **antibiotics** and blood banks.

Some inventions may play a bigger role in our lives now than they did then. The electronic computer, color television, magnetic tape, synthetic rubber, and Velcro were all pioneered in the 1940s. Designers and architects applied the forward-looking, scientific feeling to everything from toasters to office buildings. The new fashion seemed to signal the beginnings of a more modern era.

ENIAC

The first large-scale electronic digital computer was unveiled on February 14, 1946 *(above)*. The machine, standing 24 m (80 ft.) long and 5.4 m (18 ft.) high, was called the Electronic Numerical Integrator and Computer (ENIAC). It weighed 27 t (30 tn.) and contained 17,468 vacuum tubes to handle calculations.

The Pentagon

Completed in 1943, the huge five-sided complex known as the Pentagon *(above)* is the largest office building in the world. As the new home of the Department of Defense, it became the nerve center of the nation's war effort. The Pentagon sits on 13.6 hectares (34 acres), contains 27 km (17 mi.) of corridors, and is the workplace today of more than 25,000 employees.

The United Nations

Postwar architecture stressed simplicity in design. The Secretariat Building of the United Nations in New York City *(below)* was the first skyscraper whose tower was conceived as a single shaft from top to bottom.

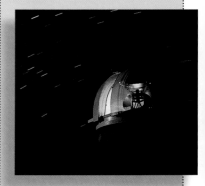

Eye on the Sky

On nearly every clear night since it was first installed in 1948, scientists have scanned the skies using the 508-cm (200-in.) Hale Telescope at the Palomar Observatory in southern California *(above)*. The huge telescope's moving parts weigh about 477 t (530 tn.), with the mirror alone weighing 13 t (14.5 tn.).

Famous 1 FIRSTS

The Transistor

Perhaps the most significant invention of the 1940s was the transistor. First demonstrated on December 23, 1947, the tiny electrical conducting devices are now at the heart of most electronic machines.

Instant Pictures

In 1947, Edwin Land *(below)* announced a new photographic process that produced a picture in one minute. Though some people dismissed the new invention as a gimmick, the film's instant images made Polaroid Land cameras a big hit with the public.

Breaking the Sound Barrier

During World War II, when American jets reached speeds of 872 km/h (545 mph), near the speed of sound, they became hard to control, shook violently, and sometimes broke apart. From this experience, some believed the **sound barrier** could not be broken. But on October 14, 1947, air force major Chuck Yeager *(right)* piloted his rocket-powered plane to a speed of 1,117 km/h (698 mph), becoming the first person to move at **supersonic** speed.

Molds and Bacteria Save Lives!

Though discovered in 1928, the antibiotic penicillin, which is made from *Penicillium* spores *(below, left),* was first put to practical use during World War II *(left),* fighting pneumonia, gangrene, and other infections. In 1944, researchers developed streptomycin from *Streptomyces* microbes *(below, right).* This powerful antibiotic soon began to win the battle against tuberculosis.

People Dr. Charles Drew

Before Dr. Charles Drew developed a way to collect and store blood **plasma,** blood **transfusions** went directly from one person to another. His breakthrough allowed for the creation of blood banks, where blood could be kept and used whenever necessary. As head of the blood banking program in Great Britain, Dr. Drew and his team *(right)* saved thousands of lives during the war.

Dr. Drew, an African American, then returned to the United States to direct the American Red Cross Blood Bank. When the U.S. Army decided to **segregate** the blood of black and white soldiers, he protested. He stated that "there is absolutely no scientific basis for any difference [in blood] according to race." But the government and the army disagreed, and Dr. Drew was relieved of his post.

Fighting against Fear

After suffering through the pain of the Great Depression and World War II, Americans were ready for change. Happily, the 1950s brought low **unemployment,** higher incomes, and new prosperity.

The bright economic news was dimmed by the fear of **nuclear war** and the spread of **Communism,** however. And while black and white soldiers fought side by side in Korea, more than half of the African-American families at home lived in poverty. Even the most successful blacks were denied equal opportunities in housing, jobs, and education. Nonviolence became a tool for change as African Americans joined together in protest over civil-rights issues. A movement that would change the future of America was growing in strength.

Living with the Bomb

When the Soviet Union's first hydrogen bomb exploded, Americans faced a new fear—the possibility of nuclear war. Many people built backyard bomb shelters and stocked them with food, water, **Geiger counters,** and survival tools. Schoolchildren practiced **"duck-and-cover" drills** (right) to prepare for air raids. Civil defense manuals and government pamphlets assured the public that "your chances of living through an atomic attack are much better than you thought."

Linda's Landmark Case

Linda Brown *(above)*, like many black children, went to a **segregated** school miles from her home, because her neighborhood school was for whites only. Linda's father sued the Topeka, Kansas, school board. The case went all the way to the U.S. Supreme Court, which ruled that separating children into schools based on race was **unconstitutional.**

The Forgotten War

In 1950, Communist North Korea attacked non-Communist South Korea. Surprised by the invasion, South Korea was almost overrun. When the United Nations sent troops into action, supported by U.S. forces, President-elect Eisenhower visited troops in the field *(right)*. By the war's end in 1953, about 600,000 soldiers had died. The border between North and South Korea was restored, and the two nations returned to their former ways of life.

People Joseph McCarthy

In 1950, Wisconsin senator Joseph McCarthy (1908-1957) claimed that the U.S. State Department employed 200 members of the Communist Party. The claim was untrue, but the public demanded action. McCarthy headed a committee in Congress that investigated suspected Communists. During the hearings, many innocent people were wrongly accused. By 1954, the public realized that McCarthy had gone too far. The hearings ended, and McCarthy was shunned by his fellow congressmen. Historians coined the term "McCarthyism" to describe this type of unfair investigation.

Flags

Hawaii

Alaska

For nearly 50 years, the United States had only 48 states. In 1959, Alaska and Hawaii were added, bringing the total to 50. The Hawaiian Islands are tiny, but Alaska's land area is nearly one-fifth that of the entire nation. It is our largest state!

Big Breakthroughs

The 1950s saw major advances in science and technology—a **vaccine** for **polio,** the first human kidney transplant, and a heart-lung machine that did the work of both organs during surgery. Atomic energy found a peacetime use, as the first nuclear power plant produced electricity in Idaho. The power of computers continued to grow, as more components and programs were developed.

Perhaps the biggest news came in the race to explore space. The Soviets were first into space with their satellites *Sputnik I* and *II.* The United States soon followed with *Explorer I.* In 1958, the National Aeronautics and Space Administration (NASA) was established, and it named its first team of astronauts the following year. In the meantime, animal astronauts were our first space explorers.

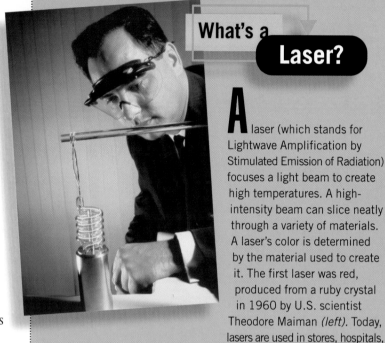

What's a Laser?

A laser (which stands for Lightwave Amplification by Stimulated Emission of Radiation) focuses a light beam to create high temperatures. A high-intensity beam can slice neatly through a variety of materials. A laser's color is determined by the material used to create it. The first laser was red, produced from a ruby crystal in 1960 by U.S. scientist Theodore Maiman *(left).* Today, lasers are used in stores, hospitals, factories, and classrooms.

Catching Up to *Sputnik*

Early space race stars were the U.S. "astrochimps" and the Soviet satellite, *Sputnik.*

WHAT THE MONKEYS' RIDE TELLS US AND PLANS FOR MAN IN SPACE

BIG RIDDLE FOR THE U.S. FAMILY: WHERE DOES THE MONEY GO?

LIFE

AMERICA'S SPACE TRAVELERS: ABLE AND BAKER

JUNE 15, 1959

Before October 4, 1957, many Americans thought the United States was superior to the Soviet Union in technology. That idea was shattered when the Soviets successfully launched the first man-made satellite into space. Weighing only 184 pounds, *Sputnik (left)* caught the United States by surprise. The space race had its first winner!

Before humans, space travelers included mold spores, insects, mice, dogs, and monkeys. Since monkeys were most like humans, they played an important role in testing life-support systems. Test

Would You Believe?

flights also helped ground crews practice countdowns, monitoring, and recovery operations. In 1959, the monkeys Able and Baker *(far left)* were the first living creatures to return safely to earth from space.

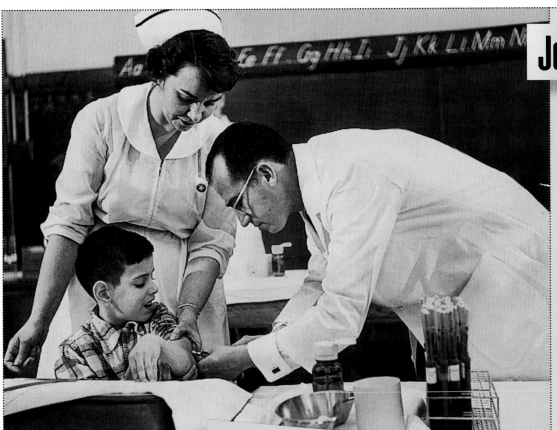

Jonas Salk

Highly **contagious, polio** struck without warning—often during the summer months. News of an outbreak closed pools and theaters, as anxious parents kept their children indoors. No one knew how the crippling disease spread, although it had been studied for years. Jonas Salk *(left)* was the first to develop a safe and successful vaccine. After injecting himself and other scientists, Salk held public tests. In 1955, the government approved the vaccine, and polio began to disappear.

People

Grace Hopper

Naval officer Grace Murray Hopper (1906-1992) wrote the first computer compiler in 1952. Her program translated human programming instructions into a code that computers could understand. Hopper also helped to develop several computer programming languages, including COBOL, which was used for UNIVAC, the first commercial computer *(right).*

Let's c o m p a r e

This Is No Desktop Computer

In 1951, UNIVAC (Universal Automatic Computer) was the first computer developed for nonmilitary use. It was also the first to store data on magnetic storage tape instead of punched cards. UNIVAC filled a room and weighed 0.72 t (8 tn.)—more than the weight of four minivans. What did it cost? A cool one million dollars!

Polio Braces

Before there was a successful vaccine, children and adults who contracted polio suffered nerve and muscle damage. Many people recovered but spent the rest of their lives using crutches or wearing leg braces, like those shown above.

The Golden Age of Television

Family Fare

At the start of the **decade,** only 9 percent of the American public owned televisions—about four million sets. By the decade's end, that figure had jumped to 86 percent—about 46 million sets. Early on, entire blocks of the day were filled with TV test patterns. By mid-decade, quiz shows, police dramas, variety shows, westerns, comedies, and kids' programs filled the airwaves.

Television reflected the decade's values. It presented idealized images of life in suburbia, where Dad worked and Mom stayed home. Few, if any, minorities were featured, and a show's success was determined by its advertising sponsors. One government spokesman noted, "Make no mistake about it. Television is here to stay. It is a new force unloosed in the land."

The Nat King Cole Show

Nat "King" Cole was the first black performer to host a network variety series. Cole's show was dropped in midseason when advertisers—fearing **boycotts** of their products by southern viewers—stopped sponsoring it.

The Power of Television

Who Won the Debate?

In 1960, about 75 million Americans watched the first televised presidential debate between John F. Kennedy and Richard M. Nixon.

Voters who watched the debate on TV said the tan, handsome JFK won. Radio listeners thought Nixon was the winner.

Leave It to Beaver

Making its debut in 1957, *Leave It to Beaver* ran for 234 episodes. The Cleaver boys never had any problems that their father, Ward, or mother, June, couldn't help them solve.

Perry Mason

Mystery and courtroom drama combined to make *Perry Mason* one of TV's most popular series.

The Mickey Mouse Club

Each day, the Mouseketeers sang and danced between Disney's Mickey Mouse cartoons.

Dragnet

Almost 38 million viewers tuned in weekly to see police cases dramatized on *Dragnet*.

People   Lucille Ball

Seen worldwide in reruns decades after its 1951 debut, *I Love Lucy* continues to sit in first place. It was the first **sitcom** to be filmed in front of a live audience, the first to have reruns, the first to be shot in Hollywood instead of New York, the first to be seen in 10 million homes, and one of the few shows to end its production while number one in the ratings. Lucille Ball's portrayal of a ditzy housewife opposite her real-life Cuban bandleader husband is a comedy classic—the most popular show in TV history.

Then & NOW!

Ron Howard: From Opie to Oscar

When *The Andy Griffith Show (left, top)* debuted in 1960, the six-year-old actor playing Opie was already a veteran. Ron Howard had appeared in his first movie when he was just 18 months old. In later years, Howard became a successful director of Academy Award-winning movies such as *Cocoon* and *Apollo 13*. Married to his high-school sweetheart, Howard *(left, bottom)* is known as a nice guy in a tough business.

Fifties Fads, Fins, and Fine Art

America enjoyed a period of booming economic growth in the 1950s. By 1954, the average citizen was earning a salary of $6,500 a year. Cars were more than just a means of transportation, and the average owner traded in his old model every two years. A car's gleaming grillwork, sleek tail fins, and bold colors said a lot about its owner's social status and style.

Millions of people moved to the suburbs, and Americans enjoyed bolder choices in fine art and fashion. High-school hallways rustled with the sound of crinolines bobbing under trendy poodle skirts. Blue jeans weren't just for workers—teens started to wear them every day. Hair styles ranged from conservative crew cuts to well-greased ducktails. All of these fads and fashions reflected a new postwar optimism.

Hula-Hoop It Up!

A Hula-Hoop craze swept the globe in the summer of 1958. The hoops were inexpensive and fun to use, and almost 100 million were sold in the United States alone. By the time winter arrived, the summertime craze had faded.

Jackson Pollock's Abstract Art

As the first American artist of his generation to become internationally famous, Jackson Pollock (1912-1956) was a master of abstract expressionism, a style that valued how a painting was created as much as its subject. Pollock would drip, fling, and pour paint across huge pieces of canvas spread on the floor. Sometimes he used trowels or sticks to move the paints, or he might mix in textured materials. The painting at left, titled *Number 3, 1949: Tiger,* included string and bits of cigarette as well as oil and enamel paints.

TV Dinners

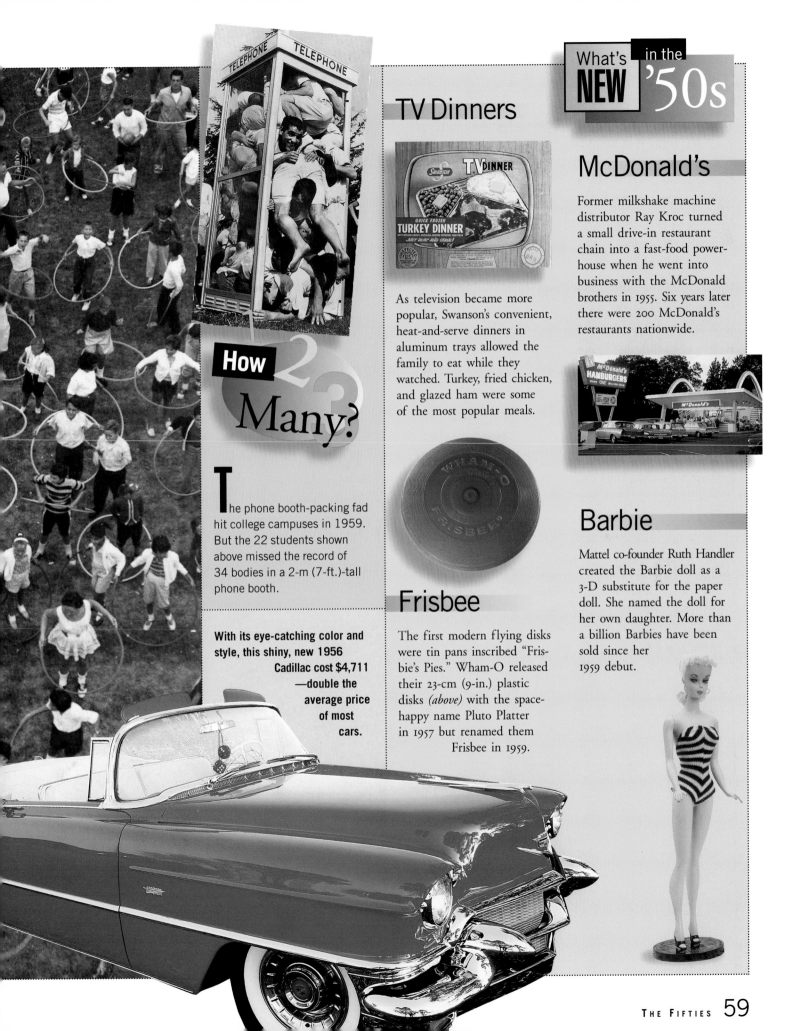

As television became more popular, Swanson's convenient, heat-and-serve dinners in aluminum trays allowed the family to eat while they watched. Turkey, fried chicken, and glazed ham were some of the most popular meals.

McDonald's

Former milkshake machine distributor Ray Kroc turned a small drive-in restaurant chain into a fast-food power-house when he went into business with the McDonald brothers in 1955. Six years later there were 200 McDonald's restaurants nationwide.

How Many?

The phone booth-packing fad hit college campuses in 1959. But the 22 students shown above missed the record of 34 bodies in a 2-m (7-ft.)-tall phone booth.

With its eye-catching color and style, this shiny, new 1956 Cadillac cost $4,711 —double the average price of most cars.

Frisbee

The first modern flying disks were tin pans inscribed "Fris-bie's Pies." Wham-O released their 23-cm (9-in.) plastic disks *(above)* with the space-happy name Pluto Platter in 1957 but renamed them Frisbee in 1959.

Barbie

Mattel co-founder Ruth Handler created the Barbie doll as a 3-D substitute for the paper doll. She named the doll for her own daughter. More than a billion Barbies have been sold since her 1959 debut.

The Best in Entertainment

In the 1950s, Americans spent more of their new wealth on **leisure** activities. As major consumers, teens made sports and music favorite forms of entertainment.

Baseball dominated the sports scene, especially three New York teams—the Yankees, Giants, and Dodgers. Then, as more Americans purchased their own televisions, all kinds of sports were broadcast—wrestling and Roller Derby had plenty of fans.

Many musical styles flourished, and record sales jumped into the millions. Dances like the stroll and the bunny hop became popular. Broadway musicals such as *The Sound of Music* and *South Pacific* drew large audiences. By mid-**decade,** rock-and-roll made its appearance, changing the music scene forever.

Althea Gibson

Breaking racial barriers in the world of tennis, Althea Gibson became the first black player to compete in the U.S. Open and to win the singles title at Wimbledon.

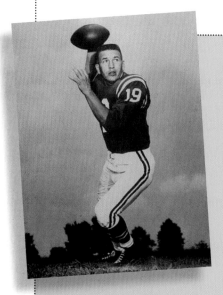

Johnny Unitas—named the greatest quarterback in the National Football League (NFL)—started his 18-year career in 1956. Two years later, he led the Baltimore Colts to a last-minute victory over the New York Giants in one of football's most exciting championships. Cool under pressure, Unitas set many NFL records and was later elected to the Pro Football Hall of Fame.

Colts' QB Johnny Unitas

Famous **1** FIRSTS

A Perfect Game

Catcher Yogi Berra leaped into the arms of Yankees pitcher Don Larsen *(left)* when he pitched the first-ever perfect postseason game in game five of the 1956 World Series.

TED WILLIAMS
Outfield BOSTON RED SOX

Baseball cards honor two stars of the game—Ted Williams of the Boston Red Sox *(far left)* and Roy Campanella of the Brooklyn Dodgers *(left)*.

Wilma Rudolph

Crippled by illness as a young child, Wilma Rudolph needed leg braces to walk. But with her family's support and her own determination, she went on to become a star athlete. At Tennessee State University, Rudolph excelled in basketball and—thanks to legendary track coach Ed Temple—earned a spot on the 1960 U.S. Olympic track team.

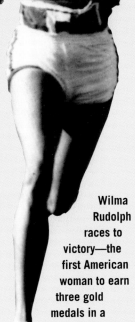

Wilma Rudolph races to victory—the first American woman to earn three gold medals in a single Olympics.

Rock-and-Roll

Chuck Berry

Known for his catchy lyrics and "duck walk" guitar moves, Chuck Berry was one of the first to compose most of his own rock-and-roll music. His hits "Maybellene" and "Roll Over Beethoven" are considered rock classics.

Elvis Presley

Known as the King of Rock-and-Roll, Elvis Presley sang and danced to a blend of rock, blues, gospel, and country. Elvis's 1956 appearance on *The Ed Sullivan Show* was watched by more than 80 percent of the national TV audience.

Dick Clark's *American Bandstand*

Beginning as a Philadelphia broadcast, *American Bandstand* went national in 1957 and became one of the longest-running variety shows in TV history. Its format of popular songs, dancing teens, and audience votes for record ratings had wide appeal. The first show devoted solely to rock-and-roll, it made its host, Dick Clark, a household name.

Other Musical Styles

Patsy Cline
Singer Patsy Cline's hits "Crazy" and "I Fall to Pieces" won over fans of country and pop music.

Miles Davis
Jazz trumpeter Miles Davis was in top form in the '50s. His quintet featured superstars such as John Coltrane and Red Garland, and pioneered the "cool" jazz style.

Harry Belafonte
Born in Harlem to Jamaican parents, Harry Belafonte made calypso music popular with hits like "The Banana Boat Song" ("Day-O").

The Sixties: Decade of Change

The 1960s were a **decade** of hope and change. John F. Kennedy, the first president born in the 20th century, called Americans to action during his inaugural speech in January 1961. And many answered his call. Young people headed out into rural America and to foreign countries to provide education and healthcare for people who desperately needed them. Others joined the armed services when the nation went to war.

Other changes in the 1960s were a lot harder for some Americans to get used to. Black Americans continued their struggle for civil rights, and people started questioning America's role in the war in Vietnam. The term "generation gap" was used to describe the differences in political viewpoints between younger and older Americans.

The Peace Corps

Established by President Kennedy in 1961, the Peace Corps sends trained Americans as "goodwill ambassadors" to developing nations. Once there, these volunteers help with agriculture, education, and health projects; small businesses; and rural engineering. By the end of the 20th century, about 140,000 Peace Corps volunteers had served in more than 100 countries.

President Kennedy and President Johnson

After his successful campaign *(top)*, John F. Kennedy (JFK) faced serious challenges as president. The most serious was when the **Cold War** almost got hot. In 1962, the Soviet Union placed missiles in Cuba, just 90 miles from Florida. President Kennedy threatened to start a war if the Soviet Union didn't back off. Luckily, however, it did.

When JFK was killed by an **assassin** in 1963, Vice President Lyndon B. Johnson took the oath of office aboard Air Force One, as Mrs. Kennedy looked on *(inset)*.

I Was There!

"I was in college when JFK created the Peace Corps, and I thought it was a great idea. I was inspired by his question, 'Ask not what your country can do for you; ask what you can do for your country.' I wanted to travel and experience a different culture, and I admired President Kennedy's idealism, so I applied. Living in another country, I learned to appreciate my own country more."
—Peace Corps volunteer (1963-1965)

The War in Vietnam

Fearing a "domino effect" of one country after another falling to **Communism**, the United States sent its first combat units to South Vietnam in 1965 to support its democratic government. The war would claim 58,000 American lives.

Antiwar Art

As thousands of men were drafted into the military, Americans began to question if the war was right. Posters like the one at right expressed one antiwar sentiment.

war is not healthy for children and other living things

Protests

A protester chooses a nonviolent way to show his opposition to the war as he confronts military police outside the Pentagon in 1967 *(above)*.

Welcome Home

Former prisoner of war Lieutenant Colonel Robert L. Stirm greets two of his children *(left)*. American forces began leaving Vietnam in 1969, with the last U.S. ground troops pulling out in 1973.

"You Have a Right to Remain Silent"

In 1966, the Supreme Court ruled in the *Miranda* v. *Arizona* case that individuals under arrest must be informed of their constitutional rights before answering questions from police.

1. You have a right to remain silent, the Constitution requires that I so inform you of this right and you need not talk to me if you do not wish to do so. You do not have to answer any of my questions.

2. Should you talk to me, anything which you might say in answer to my questions can and will be introduced into evidence in court against you.

3. If you want an attorney present at this time or any time hereafter, you are entitled to such counsel. If you cannot afford to pay for counsel, we will furnish you with counsel if you so desire.

4. Knowing your rights as I have just related them to you, are you now willing to answer my questions without having an attorney present?

The Fight for Civil Rights

African Americans' 100-year-long fight for civil rights reached a peak in the 1960s. School-children and college students, political leaders and working people used **boycotts,** marches, rallies, and strikes to bring national attention to the issues that affected their lives: **segregation** and **lynching** and unequal voting rights, employment, and education. Ultimately, this movement led to victories that would change the treatment not only of blacks, but also of women, Latinos, and other minorities.

During this movement some ordinary people rose to become great leaders. Many people were victims of racist violence, and some even lost their lives in the struggle for equality. But their sacrifices gave rise to new generations of freedom fighters for many years to follow.

People | Chavez and Huerta

Historically, farms in western states depended on a work force of mainly Chicano and Mexican migrant workers. These men, women, and children had been subject to low pay and the poorest working conditions. Led by Cesar Chavez *(left, top, center),* and volunteers like Dolores Huerta *(left, bottom),* the United Farm Workers (UFW) was founded in 1962 to serve as a voice for these laborers. Their battle cry, *Huelga!* (Spanish for "Strike!"), was a powerful call to action for produce pickers across America.

March on Washington

More than 200,000 citizens attended the 1963 March on Washington for Jobs and Freedom *(left)*, where the Rev. Dr. Martin Luther King Jr. delivered his memorable "I have a dream" speech *(above)*.

Civil Rights for All

The Civil Rights Act of 1964 outlawed whites-only policies in public places, forbade racial and gender discrimination in employment, and opened the door for further school desegregation.

Martyrs for Freedom

Martin & Malcolm

Although they differed in their approaches—Dr. King was an **integrationist,** and Malcolm X a black **nationalist**—both were killed by **assassins'** bullets.

Medgar Evers

Medgar Evers *(left)* was killed for fighting against segregation and lynchings in his home state of Mississippi.

Jack & Bobby

John and Robert Kennedy *(right)* worked for change and tolerance. They were murdered within five years of each other.

Famous **1** FIRSTS

Motley

Constance Baker Motley became the first black female New York State senator in 1964, Manhattan borough president in 1965, and a federal judge in 1966.

Chisholm

In 1968 Shirley Chisholm was the first black woman elected to Congress. In 1972, she became the first woman and first African American to run for U.S. president.

Marshall

On October 2, 1967, Thurgood Marshall, one of the 20th century's most notable legal crusaders, became the first black man to be sworn in as a justice of the U.S. Supreme Court.

Young people played a very important role in reshaping America during the 1960s. Organizations such as the Student Nonviolent Coordinating Committee (SNCC, commonly called "Snick") brought youthful energy to the civil-rights movement and, eventually, the black power movement, as young blacks became more radical in their fight against racism.

Meanwhile, the growing conflict in Vietnam spawned an antiwar movement that had particular strength on the nation's college campuses. Many students spoke out against the war, and some employed drastic measures to draw national attention to their opposition.

Over the course of the **decade,** many young people came together with determination to improve their schools and communities.

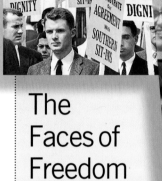

The Faces of Freedom

From Washington, D.C., where white Amherst College students picketed at the White House *(above, left)*, to Selma, Alabama, where a young marcher carried his message on his forehead *(above, right)* to the state capitol in Montgomery, brave young people of many races supported one another in the fight for equality.

How Long Must We Wait?

On February 1, 1960, four college freshmen in Greensboro, North Carolina *(above)*, bought some items at their local Woolworth's store and then sat down at the lunch counter. They were refused service because it was against store policy to serve blacks. The four remained seated until the store closed.

Over the next six months, hundreds of students joined the sit-in. By the end of the summer, the lunch counter was opened to all races.

" In his own Words "

" We asked for service and the assistant manager came over and said it was a store policy not to serve Negroes . . . that it was primarily local custom, and we said we thought it was a bad custom and something should be done about it."

—Sit-in leader Franklin McCain *(left, seated second from left)* recalling the first day of the Woolworth's sit-in

What's a Sit-in?

A sit-in is a form of nonviolent protest in which people seat themselves in an appropriate place and refuse to move until their demands are met. It is a very effective tool, too. By the end of 1961, student-led sit-ins desegregated hundreds of stores and lunch counters throughout the South.

STUDENT POWER

A New Crusade

In Birmingham, Alabama, in 1963, thousands of black teenagers led marches to end **segregation** in city stores. Police Commissioner Eugene "Bull" Connor ordered his officers to use night sticks, dogs, and fire hoses *(right)* to break up the crowds, injuring hundreds.

Despite the violence of the police, the "Children's Crusade" was a success. Birmingham business leaders finally set out a plan to end segregation in downtown stores and to hire African-American sales and office workers.

Black Power Movement

After he won his gold medal in the 1968 Olympics, U.S. sprinter Tommie Smith raised a clenched-fist salute to show his support for black unity and pride. The salute was a symbol of the black power movement, a radical philosophy of African-American self-reliance and cultural awareness. The movement appealed to young people impatient for change.

Kent State Massacre

On May 4, 1970, at Kent State University in Ohio, a student-led demonstration against the war in Vietnam erupted into violence. The Ohio National Guard fired into the crowd of protesters, killing four and wounding nine others.

The Birth of *El Movimiento*

Chicano youths and community leaders in many western states led a series of school walk-outs—like this one in Denver in 1968—to draw attention to the poor conditions that affected their schools and communities. Called "blow-outs," the rallies were organized around such issues as offering bilingual education in the classrooms, ending racist treatment in schools and public facilities, and putting a stop to police brutality in Chicano neighborhoods.

Stars for a New Generation

Throughout the 1960s, radio and television gave Americans more choices in great entertainment. Popular music had many forms, including folk songs and rhythm-and-blues, but rock-and-roll was the big favorite. American rock went overseas and came back in a British Invasion of rock groups led by the Beatles and the Rolling Stones.

Television was just about everywhere. By the end of the **decade,** 95 percent of all families had at least one set. Broadcast networks were successful with their advertiser-supported programming of entertainment, news, and sports. In 1967, Congress passed the Public Broadcasting Act to ensure that noncommercial, educational programs had a place on the television dial as well.

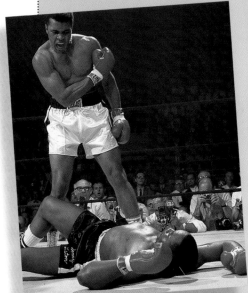

Muhammad Ali

After he defeated Sonny Liston in the first minute of their 1965 rematch *(left),* Muhammad Ali proclaimed, "I am the greatest!" Ali stuck to his beliefs in the face of harsh attacks and earned admirers worldwide.

Coach Lombardi and the Green Bay Packers

Before it was known as the Super Bowl, the first pro football championship was played between the National Football League's Green Bay Packers and the American Football League's Kansas City Chiefs in 1967. Legendary quarterback Bart Starr *(right)* led the Packers to a 35-10 victory under the leadership of the equally legendary coach Vince Lombardi *(below, left).* Lombardi was fond of saying, "Winning isn't everything—it's the only thing."

Sidney Poitier

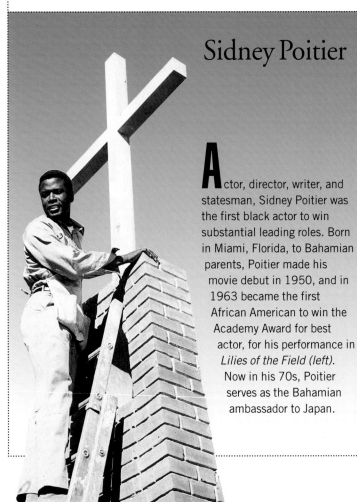

Actor, director, writer, and statesman, Sidney Poitier was the first black actor to win substantial leading roles. Born in Miami, Florida, to Bahamian parents, Poitier made his movie debut in 1950, and in 1963 became the first African American to win the Academy Award for best actor, for his performance in *Lilies of the Field (left).* Now in his 70s, Poitier serves as the Bahamian ambassador to Japan.

Music for the Head, Heart, and Soul

The Beatles

The Beatles *(below, clockwise from top)*—John Lennon, George Harrison, Paul McCartney, and Ringo Starr—put their own terrific spin on American rock and R&B, and launched a hugely successful U.S. tour in 1964. The "Fab Four" would go on to become the most famous group in rock history.

Jimi Hendrix

Seattle native and musical genius Jimi Hendrix *(above)* made the guitar the star. His screaming electric guitar licks were the roots of heavy metal.

José Feliciano

José Feliciano *(below)* grew up in New York's Spanish Harlem. His hits "High Heel Sneakers" and "Light My Fire" had Feliciano's warm vocals and Latin-influenced guitar. He earned several gold albums, Grammy Awards, and many international honors.

TV Time

The Addams Family

Based on characters created by cartoonist Charles Addams, the delightfully spooky Addams family came to TV in 1964. Gomez deliberately crashed his model trains, and Morticia cut off rose heads and displayed the thorny stems.

Jim Henson and Kermit

Jim Henson *(above with Kermit)* created the first Kermit the Frog from his mother's old coat. The Muppets appeared on a number of shows throughout the '60s. In 1969, Kermit and new Henson creations became leading cast members on *Sesame Street*.

What's in a Name?

The Motown Sound

Songwriter, businessman, and former autoworker Berry Gordy Jr. started one of America's greatest record companies with a loan of $800 from his family. Gordy named his company Motown Records for Detroit's nickname —the Motor City.

As head of a black-owned company promoting black music, Gordy signed up the most talented singers and songwriters he could find, such as the Marvelettes, and Smokey Robinson's group, the Miracles. Other Motown artists included Stevie Wonder, the Supremes *(left)*, and the Jackson Five. Berry Gordy had high standards for Motown songs— he wanted every one to be a hit. He was known to ask employees, "Would you buy this record for a dollar? Or would you buy a sandwich?" By 1966, three-quarters of Motown's hits had topped the national charts.

America Is Feelin' Groovy

In the 1960s, a lot of people were breaking new ground and breaking old rules. In the art world, a new style called pop art employed the bold graphics and techniques used for advertising to create wildly colorful pieces. In the fashion world, the sleek elegance of Jackie Kennedy and Audrey Hepburn in the early '60s gave way to the "hippie look" of gypsy skirts, love beads, granny glasses, and fringed vests at **decade**'s end.

Art and fashion were a lot of fun, but two crusaders *(opposite)* made sure that Americans took two issues very seriously: product safety and the environment. Thanks to crusaders in earlier decades *(page 12)*, our food and drugs met standards for purity and safety. It was time for our **environment** and man-made products to get a clean bill of health, too.

Mod Model Twiggy

London-based fashion designer Mary Quant won many fans with her mod (short for modern) styles. The dresses were colorful, sleek, and very short. Londoner Lesley Hornby *(left)*—nicknamed Twiggy for her slender, boyish shape—was the favorite model of mod fashion designers.

The Long and Short of It

Mini

Midi

Maxi

At the start of the century, it was considered shocking for a lady to show her ankles. But hemlines began creeping upward in the '20s and reached new heights in 1964 when miniskirts *(above, left)* stopped well above the knee. Some women preferred knee-length skirts for business wear *(above, center)*, but fashion designers offered still more choices: The "midi" skirt *(above, far right)* hit below the knee, and the "maxi" *(above, second from right)* grazed the ankle.

Warhol's Pop Art

Using modern materials and techniques, the popular, or pop, art movement shook up the traditional art world. Former commercial artist Andy Warhol created a sensation with his silkscreened prints of Campbell's soup cans *(right),* Brillo pad boxes, and other everyday objects. While experts debated whether this was art, collectors snapped up Warhol's work.

Consumer Advocate Nader

Famous for pointing out safety problems with real cars, consumer advocate Ralph Nader used a bumper car to show how collisions affect passengers. His book *Unsafe at Any Speed* claimed the auto industry put profits ahead of passenger safety. Nader raised safety questions about other products and helped launch the movement known as **consumerism.**

Art in the Landscape

One of the best-known examples of "earth art"—sculptures made from great quantities of rock and soil—Robert Smithson's *Spiral Jetty* was completed in 1970. Extending into Utah's Great Salt Lake, the piece has since been covered by rising waters.

People Rachel Carson

Noted marine biologist and author Rachel Carson (1907-1964) was one of America's first ecologists. Her carefully researched book *Silent Spring* alerted millions to the dangerous effects of pesticides on wildlife and helped focus worldwide attention on the environment. Although Carson was more comfortable exploring tidal pools than being in the public eye, she felt she had to speak out against the deadly chemicals that had "silenced the voices of spring in countless towns in America."

Claes Oldenburg

Swedish-born pop art pioneer Claes Oldenburg is known for his unusual, larger-than-life sculptures of everyday objects, like this oversize toilet. Known as soft sculptures, Oldenburg's pieces have also depicted wall fixtures, typewriters, and fast food.

The Race to Space

I n the early 1960s the National Aeronautics and Space Administration (NASA) committed itself to landing a man on the moon and safely returning him to earth by the end of the **decade.** At first, the United States lagged behind the Soviet Union in space exploration *(page 54).* But in the end, despite some mishaps and some tragic losses, NASA achieved its goal.

Preceded by a long series of spaceflight missions, the *Eagle* landed on July 20, 1969. Hundreds of millions of TV viewers watched as Neil Armstrong and Edwin "Buzz" Aldrin *(below)* became the first men to set foot on the moon, while Michael Collins awaited them in orbit above. The historic 2½-hour mission provided NASA with important lunar data, hundreds of photographs, and nearly 22.5 kg (50 lb.) of moonrocks.

The Crew of *Apollo 11*

Neil Armstrong *(above, left),* mission photographer, was so excited that mission control in Houston asked him four times to stop taking pictures in order to complete his other tasks!

" In his own Words "

"That's one small step for man, one giant leap for mankind."
—Neil Armstrong, as he stepped from the lunar lander onto the moon's surface

Spaceflight Firsts

The First American in Space

On May 5, 1961, Alan Shepard *(below, right, with President Kennedy)* completed a suborbital flight, cruising more than 160 km (100 mi.) above earth at speeds greater than 8,000 km/h (5,000 mph).

The Leader of the Pack

Three weeks before Alan Shepard's flight, on April 12, 1961, Russian cosmonaut Yuri Gagarin's A-1 booster *Vostok 1* lifted off. Less than two hours later, he completed a single orbit of earth and became the first human in space.

Among the Stars

Americans were deeply saddened when they learned that astronauts Gus Grissom, Ed White, and Roger Chaffee were killed in a launch pad fire aboard *Apollo* 1 on January 27, 1967. Theirs were the first deaths directly attributed to the U.S. space program.

By 1962, the Soviets were winning the space race. But John Glenn's historic flight on February 20 restored pride in the U.S. space program. Despite autopilot failure and mechanical difficulties, Glenn circled the globe three times in 4 hours, 55 minutes.

Around the World in a Day

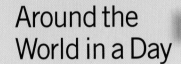

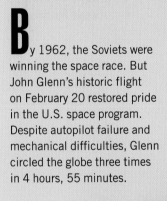

Let's Compare

Flight Data

Did you know that the average nonstop passenger flight between Washington, D.C., and Los Angeles, California, takes just about the same time as John Glenn's orbits of earth? Let's compare flight data.

Washington, D.C., to Los Angeles
Avg. flight time: 5 hr. 18 min.
Distance: 2,640 statute mi.
Speed: 555 mph
Average altitude: 37,000 ft.

John Glenn's flight in orbit
Flight duration: 4 hr. 55 min.
Distance: 75,679 statute mi.
Velocity: 17,544 mph
Altitude: 85,641,600 ft.

Star Trek

In the '60s actual space exploration was reserved for a few highly trained men. But in 1966, TV's *Star Trek* allowed viewers to "boldly go where no man has gone before" without leaving the comfort of their living rooms.

Executive Branch in Crisis

In the 1970s, President Richard Nixon had done some very good things for the country: He established diplomatic relations with China (a former enemy) and brought American troops home from Vietnam. But people were shocked when they discovered the president was involved in a terrible **scandal.** For the first time in the 20th century, a U.S. president faced losing his job because of **misconduct.**

According to our Constitution, public officials—even the president—can be removed from office through an **impeachment** process. If Congress finds enough evidence that the official broke the law, it can kick that person out of office.

Because of the Watergate scandal *(below and below, right)*, President Nixon faced serious charges but **resigned** before impeachment proceedings against him began.

What's in a Name?

The Watergate

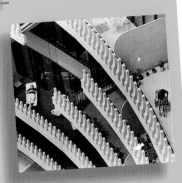

The dictionary defines "water gate" as a device, like those used in canals, that holds back water. And that kind of water gate is what a Washington, D.C., apartment and office complex *(above, right)* was named for. But when five men working for President Nixon's reelection campaign were caught breaking into their opponent's party headquarters in the Watergate complex in June 1972, the word took on a new meaning. "Watergate" was the name for the scandal—the break-in and the president's attempt to cover it up. Now, whenever there is a new political scandal, people sometimes hang the suffix "gate" after a word or name of someone involved.

Nixon Is First U.S. President to Resign

During the summer of 1973, many Americans watched a real-life drama unfold on TV. The Watergate scandal was going to cost President Richard Nixon his job.

In 1972, men working for Nixon's reelection paid burglars to install recording devices in the Democrats' offices to uncover their campaign strategy. Although Nixon did not plan the break-in, he tried to cover it up.

Senator Sam Ervin headed the Senate committee that was investigating the president. For months Nixon's staffers answered the committee's questions. At first the president tried to block the investigation. He finally decided to cooperate, but by then he had lost the trust of Congress and of the American people. Without their support, he could not lead the country. He resigned on August 9, 1974.

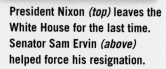

President Nixon *(top)* leaves the White House for the last time. Senator Sam Ervin *(above)* helped force his resignation.

Would You Believe?

Gerald Ford

President Gerald Ford was never elected president or vice president! President Nixon picked Ford to be vice president in 1973 when V.P. Spiro Agnew resigned. A year later, Ford replaced Nixon when he resigned.

Jimmy Carter Takes Over

When Georgia governor Jimmy Carter announced in 1974 that he would run for president, few people knew who he was. As it turned out, this helped his campaign. Many people distrusted politicians in Washington after the Watergate scandal. To them, the soft-spoken, religious Democrat from far beyond the nation's capital sounded honest.

Once he was in office, Carter's lack of Washington experience became a problem. He had a hard time getting Congress to cooperate with him—even the members of his own political party! And citizens were upset about **inflation:** Prices for food and goods kept going up and up, but people weren't earning any more money. Carter was not reelected in 1980.

"In his own Words"

"**I** want to talk to you right now about a fundamental threat to American democracy. The threat is nearly invisible in ordinary ways. It is a crisis of confidence. It is a crisis that strikes at the very heart and soul and spirit of our national will. . . . For the first time in the history of our country a majority of our people believe that the next five years will be worse than the past five years."
—Jimmy Carter, July 15, 1979

How Small? Coping with the Oil Crisis

Much of the oil for heat and gas comes from Arab countries in the Middle East. In 1960, some nations that produce and sell oil formed the Organization of Petroleum Exporting Countries (OPEC) to represent their interests.

In 1973, war broke out between Israel and the Arab nations of Egypt and Syria. OPEC's Arab members decided to stop shipping oil to Israel's allies, including the United States.

In the United States, the oil shortage forced automakers to design smaller cars that used less gas. Drivers had to wait in long lines at gas stations, and when stations ran out of gas, they posted signs *(below)* and closed early.

The Iranian Hostage Crisis

Usually people who work in an **embassy** are treated well by their host country. But things went wrong in Iran in 1979. Back in the early 1950s, the American government helped Iran's **shah**, or king, stay in power. In return, the United States got Iranian oil, and the shah kept Iran from becoming **Communist.**

Years later, an Iranian religious leader, the Ayatollah Khomeini, felt that America's influence was bad for Iran. Many people agreed and overthrew the shah in 1979. When the shah fled to the United States, angry Iranians held 66 hostages in the

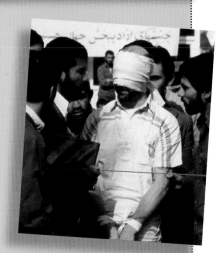

American embassy in Iran, and would free them only if President Carter sent the shah back. He refused. After 14 months of captivity, the last hostages were released in 1981.

Positive People and Contributions

Like other **decades,** the 1970s produced a good number of heroes and heroines. Jimmy Carter helped two bitter enemies work for peace. More than a million Asian refugees crossed the ocean to start new lives in America.

Athletes were doing great things, too. An 18-year-old jockey named Steve Cauthen won the Triple Crown in 1978 riding Affirmed. For achieving so much so young, *Sports Illustrated* named Cauthen sportsman of the year. Today, he owns a horse farm in Kentucky.

Puerto Rican slugger Roberto Clemente, an outfielder for the Pittsburgh Pirates, was on his way to Nicaragua with supplies for earthquake victims when he was killed in a plane crash on December 31, 1972. He later became the first Hispanic inducted into the Baseball Hall of Fame and the second baseball player featured on a U.S. postage stamp.

Arthur Ashe

Arthur Ashe was the underdog in the 1975 men's singles championship tournament at Wimbledon, England. The 31-year-old tennis star was playing Jimmy Connors, the defending champ, who was almost 10 years younger. But Ashe won, and the native of Richmond, Virginia, became Wimbledon's first African-American male champion. Years later, he wrote a history of African Americans in sports.

Who Are Boat People?

"Boat people" is the name that was given to refugees who arrived in America aboard rickety boats. These people risked their lives on the open seas when they fled their homelands, hoping for better, safer lives. Some came from Cuba and Haiti, but a great many came from Vietnam after the democratic government in South Vietnam was defeated by the **Communist** forces from North Vietnam. In 1980, a new wave of refugees came to the United States from Laos and Cambodia. Many died at sea, but more than a million are now living in the United States and have added to the **cultural diversity** of our nation.

Hammerin' Hank's Homer

Just before Henry "Hank" Aaron hit his 715th home run in 1974, he received death threats and hate mail from people who did not want a black man to break a white man's record. Still, the outfielder for the Atlanta Braves stepped up to the plate April 8 and hit one over the fence to break Babe Ruth's 1935 record. "All I could think about was that I wanted to touch all the bases," Aaron later told a reporter. "Hammerin' Hank" hit 40 more home runs before he retired after the 1976 season.

Mideast Peace

In September 1978, at Camp David, Maryland, President Jimmy Carter helped two former enemies make peace. At a conference attended by Israeli prime minister Menachem Begin, Carter, and Egyptian president Anwar Sadat *(left to right in photograph at left)*, Begin and Sadat settled some of the differences between Israel and Egypt. Israel agreed to return control of the Sinai Peninsula to Egypt; Egypt agreed to let Israel have access to the Red Sea. Their pact became known as the Camp David Accords.

People

Woodward & Bernstein

If it had not been for the hard work of two newspaper reporters, the world might never have known about the Nixon administration's involvement in the Watergate break-in *(page 74)*. Bob Woodward *(above, left)* and Carl Bernstein *(above, right)* worked for the *Washington Post*. The reporters wrote dozens of stories about the **scandal** that led to Nixon's resignation.

Woodward and Bernstein interviewed many people and read hundreds of documents to gather the facts they needed to write their stories. They also relied on information from someone who knew people in the White House. This informant's identity still remains a mystery.

The reporters' work helped the *Post* win a **Pulitzer Prize** in 1973.

How Fast?

Secretariat: Racing to New Records

In the world of horse racing, winning one of the three biggest races in a year is a great feat. But to win the Kentucky Derby, the Preakness, and the Belmont Stakes is really spectacular! In fact, it is called the Triple Crown.

In 1973, Secretariat, a reddish brown three-year-old, became the first horse in 25 years to win the Triple Crown. His Belmont Stakes run set a new world record: He ran the 1.5-mile track in 2 minutes, 24 seconds.

More Voices for Change

The civil-rights movement of the 1960s inspired other groups to demand better treatment. Native Americans tried to undo the harm caused by broken treaties and poor conditions on reservations. Some Americans became more aware of the **environment,** and of how people could injure or repair it.

And the entire country took notice when millions of women started on their quest for equality. The women's liberation movement showed how women were treated like second-class citizens, and why that should stop. Among other things, women wanted better jobs, and if women were performing the same jobs as men, they wanted the same pay. Unfortunately, unequal pay is still a problem for working women, but many women—and men—keep pushing for fairness.

American Indian Activism

Russell Means and Dennis Banks *(above)* were leaders in the American Indian Movement. In 1973, a fight over corrupt reservation leaders led to a 71-day standoff with federal marshals and the Federal Bureau of Investigation at Wounded Knee, South Dakota.

Three Mile Island Disaster

For years, Americans believed that nuclear energy plants were a clean, safe way to generate electricity. But in March 1979, an accident at the Three Mile Island power plant near Harrisburg, Pennsylvania, changed many people's minds.

The accident happened when a coolant leak exposed radio-active fuel rods in the nuclear core. If the core had gotten too hot, it would have exploded and poisoned the atmosphere with deadly radioactive particles.

Engineers at the plant were able to fix the reactor within 12 days, but frightened citizens demanded tighter government controls on nuclear power.

Earth Day

Mother Earth got her own holiday on April 22, 1970, when millions of American environmentalists celebrated Earth Day. Parades, educational seminars, and other events drew attention to the planet's fragile ecology. A few months later, the federal government created the Environmental Protection Agency. And by Earth Day's third anniversary,

the United Nations held a special conference on the environment. Caring about our blue planet became very cool.

Women who fight for equal rights are called **feminists** *(left)*. They were hopeful when Congress passed the Equal Rights Amendment (ERA) in 1972. This **constitutional amendment** would have guaranteed that women and men had the same rights. But the ERA never became law, because it wasn't approved by enough states.

People

Gloria Steinem

Gloria Steinem *(above)* has been one of the leading voices of the women's movement. In 1971, she co-founded the National Women's Political Caucus to help women enter politics. The next year, she started *Ms.* magazine and served as its editor. All 300,000 copies of the first issue sold in eight days.

Famous **1** FIRSTS

Diane Crump

Diane Crump and her horse, Fathom, may not have won the Kentucky Derby in 1970. But Crump did win a place in history as the first female jockey ever to ride in the famous race.

Play Ball!

Girls finally scored a home run in 1974 when Little League had to drop its boys-only policy. New Jersey *(above)* led the way when a judge there ruled that Little League had to allow mixed baseball teams as long as public facilities or funds were used. Not doing so violated the girls' civil rights as guaranteed in the Constitution.

No "Love" on This Court

The press called the 1973 tennis match the Battle of the Sexes. It was soon clear that the King ruled—Billie Jean King, that is *(below, left)*. When she handily beat Bobby Riggs *(below, right)* she proved that female athletes could— and should—play as tough as male athletes.

High-Tech for All

Imagine a brilliant brain, capable of performing many tasks, that fits on the tip of your finger. That is the job of a microprocessor, or microchip.

Made of silicon, a microchip contains thousands of tiny electronic components (transistors, diodes, and resistors) that work together. They understand and perform program commands, like adding up a grocery bill or giving out cash from an automatic teller.

Before microchips were around, computer systems could fill a room *(page 50)*. But with microchips inside, computers shrank to desktop size and became less expensive, so more people could own one.

Microchips were soon being used in all sorts of equipment, such as video games, cars, and wrist watches. Americans coined the phrase "high-tech" to describe the high level of technology in their daily lives.

The Right Connections

The foundation of any computer is its circuit board. This is a flat piece of insulated metal upon which microprocessors and other electronic pieces are mounted (or etched) and connected to one another with thin pieces of wire.

Steven Jobs

Stephen Wozniak

Computers Go Home

Steven Jobs and Stephen Wozniak were only in their 20s when they were tinkering in Jobs's dad's garage in Mountain View, California. They ended up designing one of the first mass-produced personal computers, the Apple II, in 1977.

Their invention was cheap and easy to use, and small businesses, schools, and individuals began gobbling up Apples. Jobs and Wozniak were running one of the country's fastest-growing companies and had helped start the personal-computer revolution.

Mariner 9 Visits Mars

Red but Not Dead

For centuries, fiery red Mars has fascinated humankind. Some imagined another race of beings living there (page 36). Others wanted to colonize the planet. But nobody really knew for sure what the Martian surface looked like. So in 1971, the United States and the Soviet Union launched space probes to answer the age-old question.

On December 2, the Soviet spacecraft, Mars 2, landed on the red planet in the midst of a raging dust storm. Within seconds, the craft was dead.

America's Mariner 9 had better luck, since it was designed to take photographs from orbit. It assumed orbit on November 13. When the storms subsided in January, the probe was able to take thousands of revealing pictures of deep canyons and four huge volcanoes. Many people agreed with the famous American astronomer Carl Sagan when he said, "Mars may be red, but it certainly isn't dead."

Calculator

When pocket calculators were invented in the '60s, only scientists and engineers used them. In 1974 a chip was designed that could do the work of six, and calculators became much smaller and cheaper. In one year the price dropped from $400 to less than $100. Now you might even get one as a gift from your bank!

Videocassette Recorder

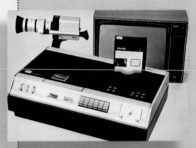

Like pocket calculators, videocassette recorders (VCRs) were products of the '60s that became popular in the '70s. To record a movie or TV show, a VCR uses several tape heads that read, then "write" audio and video tracks onto magnetic tape. Soon after the introduction of the VCR almost everyone in America could watch movies at home instead of in the theater.

What's a Catalytic Converter?

In the 1970s, engines on cars, buses, and trucks created lots of smog, a combination of smoke and fog (below, right) that was bad for people's lungs. To fight the nation's air pollution problem, Congress required auto manufacturers to control harmful **emissions.** Carmakers installed catalytic converters on all new cars.

Catalytic converters are devices that make harmful, polluting gases less harmful. The converter runs exhaust fumes from the engine through hundreds of tiny, metal-coated tubes. The heat and exposure to metal alter the molecular structure of the gases, and cleaner exhaust leaves the tailpipe. Now we can all breathe a little easier!

The Walkman

When the Sony Walkman came out in 1979, walking, running, commuting—and even vacuuming the rug— became a musical experience! Before the Japanese company introduced personal portable stereos, people on the go used transistor radios. But one heard only what the stations played. The Walkman allowed a listener the choice of a favorite tape, as well as better sound.

A Decade of Blockbusters

Bigger was definitely better in the 1970s. Americans watched breathlessly as two new skyscrapers gained and then lost first place as the world's tallest building within three years. Television networks pulled in big ratings with situation comedies and dramatic miniseries. And movie hits like *Star Wars* and *The Godfather* kept box-office cash registers ringing.

Scary movies continued to pack theaters. In 1975, *Jaws,* Steven Spielberg's thriller about man-eating sharks, had folks afraid to go in the water. And Frank Langella's romantic portrayal of Dracula in 1979 made women long for a pain in the neck.

African-American filmmakers and stars made action flicks like *Shaft* and *Superfly.* Their success helped Hollywood begin to appreciate the size and importance of the black moviegoing market.

How old is man? Ask Richard Leakey — Sybil's shrink diagnoses a rapist with 10 personalities — Body Snatchers prev. Brooke Adams

People weekly

JANUARY 8, 1979 · 75¢

It's SUPERMAN!

And It's Chris Reeve in the cape because McQueen was too fat, Stallone too Italian, Redford too expensive and Eastwood too busy

Superman Flies Again

In 1978, audiences flocked to see *Superman,* the first full-length film about the Man of Steel. They loved the classic good looks of leading man Christopher Reeve, and his performance was—well, super! The cast also included Marlon Brando as Jor-el (Superman's Kryptonian father), and Margot Kidder as reporter Lois Lane. And actor Gene Hackman nearly stole the show in his role as the arch-villain, Lex Luthor.

Martial Artist

People
George Lucas

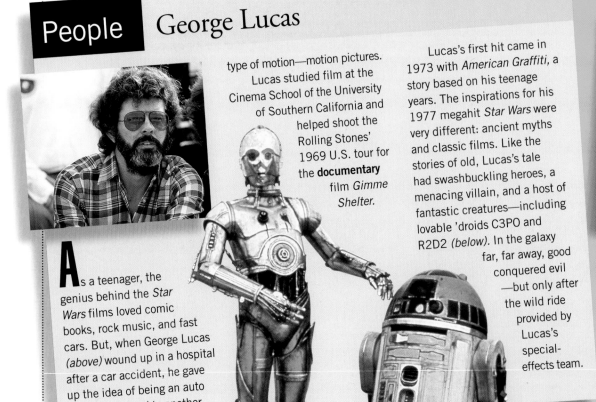

As a teenager, the genius behind the *Star Wars* films loved comic books, rock music, and fast cars. But, when George Lucas *(above)* wound up in a hospital after a car accident, he gave up the idea of being an auto racer and turned to another type of motion—motion pictures. Lucas studied film at the Cinema School of the University of Southern California and helped shoot the Rolling Stones' 1969 U.S. tour for the **documentary** film *Gimme Shelter.*

Lucas's first hit came in 1973 with *American Graffiti,* a story based on his teenage years. The inspirations for his 1977 megahit *Star Wars* were very different: ancient myths and classic films. Like the stories of old, Lucas's tale had swashbuckling heroes, a menacing villain, and a host of fantastic creatures—including lovable 'droids C3PO and R2D2 *(below).* In the galaxy far, far away, good conquered evil —but only after the wild ride provided by Lucas's special-effects team.

Chinese-American movie star Bruce Lee *(above)* punched, kicked, and whirled his way through martial arts movies until his sudden death at the age of 32. Fans still admire Lee's graceful style. He helped make martial arts really popular in the United States.

Past and Present for TV Fans

The 1974 hit comedy series *Chico and the Man* was a story about how Chico, a hip young Chicano played by Freddie Prinze *(right)*, became partners with Ed Brown, a crusty old Anglo man played by Jack Albertson *(far right)*. Although they were of different cultures and **generations,** the two men became friends while working in Ed's run-down Los Angeles garage.

Chico and the Man

School's Cool on *Welcome Back, Kotter*

In 1975, comedian Gabriel Kaplan *(above, left)* played Gabe Kotter, a man who returns to his high school as a teacher. He helped the "Sweathogs" get good grades: even the not-so-smart Vinnie Barbarino, played by a young John Travolta *(above, right)*.

Happy Days

With his leather motorcycle jacket, blue jeans, and thumbs-up sign, Arthur "The Fonz" Fonzerelli, played by Henry Winkler *(right)*, was the undisputed King of Cool in *Happy Days*. Viewers liked the comedy's look at life in the simple times before the challenges of the Vietnam War and Watergate.

How Tall?

Sears Tower: World's Tallest Building

In 1974, the Sears Tower in Chicago, Illinois, beat out New York's Twin Towers as the world's tallest. All three were 110 stories high, but the Sears Tower was 31.5 m (104 ft.) taller.

An Indian-American engineer named Fazlur Khan designed Sears, Roebuck and Co.'s sleek headquarters. To reduce the amount of steel used, and to help brace the building against Chicago's high winds, Khan used "bundled tubes"—groups of narrow steel cylinders gathered into thick columns.

Roots: One Family's Saga

The family history of Alex Haley *(right, top)* became a best-selling book and one of the most-watched shows in TV history.

The book *Roots* was based in part on stories that Haley's grandmother had told him as a child. In January 1977, 130 million people watched the miniseries *Roots (right, bottom)*, the story of how Haley's African ancestors struggled for freedom in the American South. Later that year, the book received a special **Pulitzer Prize.** Haley inspired many others to uncover their own roots.

Dance to the Music

In the 1970s, rock music evolved into a variety of styles. The Eagles played country rock, while groups like Aerosmith and Led Zeppelin played hard rock. It was also the **decade** of the supergroup: Earth, Wind & Fire's melodic sounds were produced by a group of nine men.

But when people think of '70s music, they think of disco, music designed to make people dance. Born in New York discotheques, or dance clubs, the style had a more danceable beat than most rock music. It was hard to be still if Van McCoy was telling you to "Do the Hustle!" or Chic was singing "Freak Out!"

By 1978, most musicians had cut a disco record, including rock legends the Rolling Stones and soul singer Marvin Gaye. Even musical innovator Frank Zappa tried it: His hit single "Dancin' Fool" made fun of the entire disco culture.

Bruce Springsteen: Born to Be Boss

From the moment the first guitar chords of "Born to Run" thundered from the radio in 1975, it was clear that this guy from New Jersey hadn't been playing the guitar since he was 13 for nothing. Bruce Springsteen and his E Street Band were glory bound. Springsteen wrote songs about people and situations that were easy to understand. Most of Springsteen's songs were about hardworking people, and his fans called him the Boss. He was really "in charge" of rock-and-roll!

A Knight in Shining Polyester

Travolta Had the Fever

The movie *Saturday Night Fever* made disco a national craze in 1977. The movie soundtrack sold 30 million copies. And, like John Travolta's character *(left)*, Americans hit the discos to boogie the night away under sparkling mirrored balls. Disc jockeys kept the beat coming with songs such as the Bee Gees' "Stayin' Alive" and Yvonne Elliman's "If I Can't Have You."

Salsa Beat Adds Some Latin Spice

Salsa ("sauce" in Spanish) is a term used to describe one style of Latin music, and the dancing that goes with it *(right)*.

Its lively sound is rooted in *son*, dance music popular in Cuba, Puerto Rico, and Africa in the 1940s. During the next decade, Cuban and Puerto Rican immigrants brought son to the mainland United States. Over time, son and other Latin styles were grouped under the name

What's Salsa?

"salsa." By the 1970s, it was the dominant pop music in Latino communities in the United States and Latin America.

Movin', Groovin' Jackson 5

One of music's most talented families took the world by storm in the '70s. Jackie, Tito, Jermaine, Marlon, and Michael Jackson put out a dozen irresistible hits including "I Want You Back," "ABC," and "Never Can Say Goodbye."

The Jackson Five was part of a family of nine kids. Three girls—Rebbie, La Toya, and Janet—each made their own records, and Randy later joined his brothers.

Many fans admired the clean-cut, close-knit Jacksons. In 1972, Congress commended the group for "contributions to American youth."

Shocking Kiss

Hard-rock band Kiss was famous for their wild shows, which featured bassist Gene Simmons's fire-breathing theatrics. Hardly anyone ever saw the band members, who had a hit in 1975 with "Rock and Roll All Nite," without their signature makeup.

We Want the Funk

Parliament/Funkadelic (left), George Clinton's megagroup, served up some of the decade's hippest, most adventurous music. The band put on amazing shows with musicians in outlandish costumes and Clinton landing on stage in a spaceship. Truly, this was funk!

Punk and New Wave Make a Big Splash

In the '60s and '70s musicians created a new rock music style. They played "punk" music that was loud and fast. New wave bands like the B-52's (above) used high-tech **synthesizers** (as well as "old-fashioned" guitars) to blend punk with pop.

New Style Directions

Many of the hippest fashions of the 1990s were just as hip two **decades** earlier. Kids in the 1970s wore the same platform shoes and overalls, and the flannel shirts and work boots that defined the '90s "grunge" look.

Some hair styles that were all the rage then are still around. The short, sleek bobs that many women wear are updated versions of a style first popularized by a young ice skater named Dorothy Hamill. People liked her "wedge" haircut almost as much as her gold-medal performance at the 1976 Winter Olympics.

But some styles of the '70s did not survive the decade. Men's "leisure suits," belted jackets and pants made out of polyester knit, have not made a comeback. Nor have the incredibly short shorts known as "hot pants."

Getting That Wing Thing

A TV star's haircut was the hot style in 1976. Women and girls poured into salons and asked stylists to give them "feathers" or "wings."

Farrah Fawcett introduced her new hairdo on the show *Charlie's Angels.* The ex-model's silvery blonde mane featured short layers around her face that were brushed forward, then blown back with a hand-held blow-dryer. The layers were called feathers because each piece was easy to see, like the feathers on a bird.

Let's Compare

Do You Have Sole?

Shoes got funkier and chunkier in the '70s. Platforms *(right)* and clogs made you taller, whereas the sturdy Earth Shoe *(below)* held your heel lower than your toes.

Famous 1 FIRSTS

Johnson Breaks Color Barrier

In 1974, Beverly Johnson earned a place in fashion history as *Vogue* magazine's first black cover model. Since so many people think *Vogue* has the best coverage of beauty and high fashion, it was great to see that black women could be accepted as beautiful, too.

Being a cover girl was nothing really new for Johnson. She was attending Northeastern University on a full scholarship when she appeared on the cover of *Glamour.*

"When I started being on the cover, white Southern readers—for the first time—said that they wanted to be me," she told a *Glamour* writer. "Black models never had that positive a reaction before. Maybe the world had evolved."

Can't Get Enough Healthy Stuff

Crazy about Running and Crunching

In the 1970s, more Americans started thinking about healthful foods and physical fitness. People started eating foods that were new to them, such as granola (a crunchy cereal made of oats, honey, and brown sugar, and sometimes dried fruits and nuts), brown rice, and bean sprouts or alfalfa sprouts. People took up jogging and read self-help books to help them have healthy minds to go with their healthy bodies.

Try it!

Yoga: Lotus Position

Many Americans learned about Asian philosophies in the '70s. One of the most popular was yoga, which was developed in India about 5,000 years ago. People who practice yoga exercise their bodies in a variety of positions, such as the lotus (above). To do a half lotus, sit up straight on a mat or rug and cross your legs. Bend your left knee and pick up your left foot, then put it as high on your right thigh as you can. To go for the full lotus, drop your left knee to the floor, lift your right foot and place it on your left thigh.

Must-Have Gizmos and Goodies

CB Radios

Before car phones, drivers had CB, or Citizens Band, radios. Truckers used the electronic transmitters during the energy crisis to tell one another where gas was available. On the air, CBers used a "handle," or nickname. In fact, they had a whole language. "Smokey Bear" was a police officer; "Smokeys with ears" were police with their own CBs.

Pet Rocks

A Pet Rock (left) was the gift to give during the 1975 holiday season. For $3.95, you got a small, obedient "pet," a carrying case, and an owner's manual with housebreaking tips and tricks any rock could learn.

Happy Faces

It was hard to get through the '70s without seeing this yellow happy face. "Smiley" was on everything, from notebooks to political bumper stickers.

Dawn and Co.

Barbie too big for you? Then try Dawn for size. Topper's 6-inch-tall, blue-eyed blonde and her 18 pals were popular between 1970 and 1973. Girls liked Dawn and her friends partly because their smaller size made them easier to carry than larger fashion dolls.

Conservatism In Control

During the 1980s, many politicians were elected on their promise of less government and more opportunities for private enterprise. They appealed to political conservatives who thought that the federal government was too big, too expensive, and too inefficient.

To them, Ronald Reagan was a hero. Elected president in 1980, he promised to scale back government intervention and encouraged businesses to pick up where Uncle Sam left off. Reagan also called for more money for the country's Defense Department, to ensure military superiority over "the evil empire," or the Soviet Union. His successor, George Bush, also adopted a conservative approach when he was elected in 1988.

First Lady Says: "Just Say No!"

Wives of presidents often make certain social issues their special projects. For example, first lady Nancy Reagan (left) decided she would tackle the nation's growing drug problem.

In 1983, she launched her "Just Say No" to drugs campaign. Because Mrs. Reagan really wanted to reach kids, she visited schools. There she tried to spread the word about how drugs ruin the lives of users and their families.

People — Sandra Day O'Connor

In September 1981, the U.S. Supreme Court got its first female judge, Sandra Day O'Connor (below, with Chief Justice Warren Burger). President Reagan appointed O'Connor to replace Justice Potter Stewart, who was retiring. Now a woman would be able to interpret and apply the law of the land.

O'Connor had worked hard to reach the nation's highest court. In 1952, she graduated from Stanford Law School at the top of her class. But when she interviewed with law firms, they only offered her secretarial jobs.

"Women's equality under the law does not effortlessly translate into equal participation in the legal profession," she recalled in 1985.

O'Connor became a lawyer in the Arizona attorney general's office and later a judge in that state before she went to the federal court.

Aiding Contras Causes Scandal

The Iran-Contra **scandal** of the mid-'80s rocked the Reagan administration. Members of the president's staff secretly raised money to help rebels in Nicaragua overthrow their nation's **Communist** government. His staffers did this even though Congress had outlawed all aid to the rebels, or contras, in 1984.

The staff members raised the money by selling surplus U.S. arms to Iran. In return, Iran agreed to persuade terrorists in Lebanon to free seven American hostages.

Stories about this illegal operation gradually came out. Those involved, like U.S. Marine lieutenant colonel Oliver North (above, right), testified before Congress in 1987. He

Lt. Col. Oliver North

and others were convicted of wrongdoing, but an appeals court overturned the convictions on a technicality. Reagan insisted he knew nothing about the operation and avoided getting into trouble.

Ronald Reagan

Ronald Reagan *(left)* was one of America's most popular presidents. The former governor of California was called the Great Communicator for his terrific ability to deliver a message.

Reagan learned a lot about public speaking as a film actor. He had starred in numerous films, including *Bedtime for Bonzo*, in which one of his co-stars was a chimp *(below)*.

In 1982, Samantha Smith *(above, center)* wrote a letter to Soviet premier Yuri Andropov. He was so impressed that he brought her to his country for two weeks. The 10-year-old diplomat showed that kids can make a difference. Here's part of her letter.

"I have been worrying about Russia and the United States getting into a nuclear war. Are you going to vote to have a war or not? God made the world for us to live together in peace and not to fight."

Sadly, Smith and her father died in a plane crash in 1985.

Dangerous Attacks on the Environment

Garbage Barge

For two months in 1987, the crew aboard the barge *Mobro 4000 (below)* wandered at sea because nobody would accept their smelly cargo—2,790 t (3,100 tn.) of garbage. In the end, the cargo was burned in its home state of New York.

Surf's Gross!

Beachgoers on the East Coast discovered they were sharing the sand with garbage during the summer of 1988. The scariest trash included medical waste, such as hypodermic needles. The beach did clear up, but not entirely.

Deadly Oil Spill

The worst oil spill in U.S. history happened in March 1989 when the *Exxon Valdez* ran aground and leaked about 41.8 million l (11 million gal.) of crude oil into Alaska's Prince William Sound. The spill killed animals and contaminated the shoreline.

Business Boom and Bust

With a pro-business president in the White House, private enterprise was encouraged to grow in the 1980s. College students studied business management and were rewarded with high-paying jobs when they graduated. The term "yuppies" was coined to describe the "young urban professionals"—men and women who wore the new uniform of dark suits, crisp shirts, and red silk "power" ties.

Most of the young professionals were affected by at least one corporate **merger.** Between 1980 and 1988, more than 25,000 mergers and buyouts took place, worth some two trillion dollars. But there were bad economic times as well. Prices on the stock market plunged in 1987 *(below)*, recalling the crash of 1929. Prices were climbing again by the end of the '80s.

Merger Mania

Imagine that you own a company and want to buy another one. But either you don't have enough money to pay for it or you'd rather not spend the money you do have to buy it. What do you do?

In the '80s, you might have managed to buy it through a leveraged buyout. Simply put, one corporation borrows some money (using its assets as collateral) and buys the second company. In many cases, the corporation would break up the company it just bought into smaller companies, keep the parts it liked, close down others, and sell off the rest to pay off the loan.

If everything went according to plan, the new corporation would have new products or services to sell, and it would have gotten rid of some of its competition at the same time. The bad part was that a lot of jobs were usually lost in the process.

Black Monday: The Crash of '87

On Monday, October 19, 1987, the stock market crashed. Stock prices fell 22.6 percent —almost twice as much as they had dropped in 1929. Traders *(below)* watched as 604.5 million shares of stock—more than double the record—were sold on "Black Monday."

Some experts blamed the crash on inflated stocks; a company's stock was too expensive when compared with how much money the company actually earned. Others said it was the fault of the government for racking up too much debt and making foreign investors nervous.

24-Hour News and Grooves

Until 1980, TV programming was limited to three national networks (CBS, NBC, and ABC) and a handful of local stations. With the exception of HBO (Home Box Office), there wasn't much on cable.

A businessman from Georgia named Ted Turner helped change that. On June 1, 1980, he launched CNN (Cable News Network) as the first 24-hour news channel. His news team provided coverage of events from around the world, which they then delivered to cable providers via satellite.

And in August 1981, former radio executives created MTV (Music Television). They knew that advertisers wanted to reach young people, who loved rock

music. So they decided to run music videos on a cable channel. Pretty soon, a song could be seen, not just heard.

Homelessness on the Rise

In the '80s America was facing a new crisis: men, women, and children who had no place to live. A great number of homeless adults had lost their jobs because of layoffs or corporate mergers. Once they lost their paychecks, they could not pay rent and had to move onto the streets.

More fortunate Americans gave time and money to help the homeless with temporary shelters and blankets. But at the end of the century, there were still thousands without permanent homes.

Students against Apartheid

American college students *(below)* took a stand against South Africa's racist apartheid government in the '80s by demanding that their schools stop investing in companies that did business there. This was called divestiture because schools were asked to divest themselves of such holdings.

In 1948, South Africa's white minority adopted a policy of "apartheid," their word for racial separation. Blacks had to attend inferior schools, live in horrible slums, and use pass-books to move about in their own country.

The injustice of apartheid bothered students in the United States. Knowing that the South African government could not survive long without foreign investment, the students and other organizations demanded that American businesses get out of South Africa until blacks got an equal voice in ruling their country *(page 117)*.

Would **You** *Believe?*

The One and Only Phone Company

Before 1982, almost all Americans used one telephone company —AT&T (American Telephone and Telegraph Co.). They made phones and provided local and long-distance service.

As far back as 1909, the government claimed AT&T had a **monopoly** in the telephone industry. Finally, in 1982, AT&T agreed to give up its 22 regional companies, but kept its manufacturing and long-distance businesses.

Science Triumphs and Tragedies

Science news was very mixed during the 1980s. On the positive side, there were great advances in personal computing. In the medical field, a surgeon implanted the first permanent artificial heart in a patient in 1982. Though it could not keep a patient alive forever, the artificial heart became a model for others that are used to keep patients alive while they wait for heart transplants.

But the science and technology news also warned of an incurable new disease called acquired immune deficiency syndrome, or AIDS. Caused by the human immunodeficiency virus (HIV), it attacks the body's immune system, damaging its ability to fight off sickness.

The nation faced another tragedy when the space shuttle *Challenger* exploded just after takeoff. NASA promised greater safeguards for future missions.

Map labels:
San Francisco Bay
Route 280
Route 101
San Francisco
CALIFORNIA
Stanford University
PALO ALTO Xerox Parc
MOUNTAIN VIEW Netscape
LOS ALTOS
Steve Jobs's Garage
CUPERTINO
Apple
SANTA CLARA Intel
San Jose

What's in a Name?

Silicon Valley

Many of the companies that produce high-tech computer hardware and software are located in the San Francisco Bay Area. In the 1980s, the area was nicknamed Silicon Valley for all of the silicon chips that were being created there. Even though there aren't fields of silicon shimmering in the sunlight, Silicon Valley is a real place.

People Ryan White

Ryan White *(left, top)* was only 13 years old when he learned he had gotten the AIDS virus in blood products he was taking for his hemophilia, a disease he had had since birth.

In 1984, many people thought the AIDS virus *(left, bottom)* could be passed by casual contact—by shaking hands, sneezing, or coughing. Even though AIDS can't be caught that way, people in Ryan's school were scared to be near him and only let him come to class after a court battle. In 1987, Ryan's family moved to another Indiana town, where he was treated kindly. Ryan died in 1990.

Smallpox: Death of a Killer

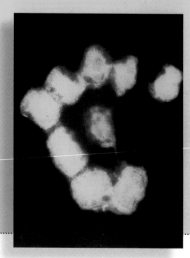

The World Health Organization (WHO) announced in 1980 that one of humankind's worst enemies had been wiped out. For centuries most people who caught the smallpox virus *(right)* died from it. WHO began its successful international vaccination campaign in 1967; by 1979, no smallpox cases had been reported.

The *Challenger*

The explosion of the space shuttle *Challenger (left)* on January 28, 1986, was one of the saddest moments in U.S. history. People all over the country watched in horror as the 25th shuttle mission blew up minutes after takeoff, killing all seven crew members. Many folks were watching the lift-off, because one of the crew wasn't a professional astronaut. Christa McAuliffe, a high-school teacher from New Hampshire, was going to teach classes from space. The lost crew *(clockwise from left rear):* Ellison Onizuka, Christa McAuliffe, Gregory Jarvis, Judith Resnik, Ronald McNair, commander Francis Scobee, and pilot Michael Smith.

How Does a Microwave Work?

"Nuking," or cooking, food in microwave ovens *(below)*, really wasn't done much in most households until the 1980s. But the technology behind it has existed since the 1940s.

Microwaves are electro-magnetic energy waves that make food molecules move fast, thereby generating heat. These waves are set into motion by a magnetron, a vacuum tube that U.S. scientists used to create smaller and better radar equipment for the Allies in World War II.

Sally Ride

On June 18, 1983, Sally Ride *(right)* became the first American woman to fly in space. The flight engineer was one of five crew members aboard the space shuttle *Challenger* on a six-day mission. She helped deploy two satellites.

Ride had considered playing professional tennis before she got her degrees in physics. She became an astronaut instead.

Famous **1** **FIRSTS**

Eighties Go for It

America's favorite TV comedy of the 1980s was the brainchild of one of the nation's best-loved funny guys. Created by Bill Cosby, *The Cosby Show* was a warm-hearted family comedy. But it was not his first television success. In 1965, Cosby became the first black actor to star in a network drama, *I Spy.* He won three Emmys for his performance in the series. Cosby also created a cartoon, *Fat Albert and the Cosby Kids,* and has had a prime-time TV show in every decade since the '60s.

Jane Fonda was another veteran performer who made it big again in the 1980s. She released a successful exercise book and video just as most households were getting their first VCRs. In addition, she appeared in *On Golden Pond,* with her father, Henry Fonda—one of America's most-beloved film and stage actors.

Maya Lin

While studying architecture at Yale University, Maya Lin *(above)* was given an interesting homework assignment. A group in Washington, D.C., wanted to create a memorial to honor the Vietnam veterans and invited people to submit designs for the monument.

Lin won the competition in 1981 with a simple yet powerful design *(above).* Engraved on the faces of two granite walls were the names of more than 58,000 Americans who either had died or were missing in action during the war. The Wall, as it is called, is now one of the most-visited monuments in Washington.

Try it!

Sushi Rolls All Over America

Although sushi has long been popular in Japan, Americans adopted the dish during the '80s. People everywhere tried the nuggets of seafood, veggies, and rice. You can eat sushi with chopsticks *(left)* or your fingers. Here's how to use chopsticks:

Step 1. Place one stick in the hand you write with, anchoring it with your thumb and resting the tip against your third finger.

Step 2. Hold the second stick like you hold a pencil.

Step 3. Move the top stick up and down to grasp pieces of food. Practice makes perfect!

1
2
3

See Jane Sweat

The fitness craze of the '70s was alive and well in the '80s. What changed was how people exercised.

In 1981, actress Jane Fonda introduced a health regimen with a book, audiotape, and videos of her aerobic workouts. Inspired by peppy music and Fonda's commands to "make it burn," women danced and crunched, hoping to look as trim as their glamorous instructor.

The Cosby Show

Beginning in 1984, NBC's *The Cosby Show* became one of the most popular situation comedies in history. Bill Cosby *(below, with Keshia Knight Pulliam)* played Dr. Cliff Huxtable, a father of five, and husband to lawyer wife Claire. The show solved the typical family problems with love, humor, and an African-American flair.

How to Be a Human Yo-Yo

Bungee jumpers tied one end of a stretchy rope, or bungee cord, to a high platform and the other end to their ankles, and jumped! It was a dare-devil's way to take a dip.

People

Keith Haring

In the 1980s, artist Keith Haring *(below)* went from painting graffiti on the walls of New York to running his own gallery and boutique. The bright colors and simple lines of his art were hugely popular, and appeared on everything from note cards to watches to album covers.

Message in the Music

In the 1960s and '70s, a lot of popular music inspired people to think about social problems like poverty, war, and pollution. In the '80s, musicians took action to help people in need.

Two great rock-and-roll charity events took place in 1984 and 1985. Musicians in the United States and Great Britain raised money to help millions of African **famine** victims. In the United States, an all-star group recorded the hit single "We Are the World" *(right)* and used the record profits to buy and deliver food to the starving people.

But there were other messages in the music. Rap music found a national audience, using spoken words over driving music to talk about life in the big city. And singers who could dance up a storm like Michael Jackson and Madonna seemed tailor-made for music videos.

How Short?

Three women helped popularize super short hair for women. Annie Lennox *(top)*, Grace Jones *(middle)*, and Laurie Anderson *(bottom)* made their buzz cuts look glamorous.

Lennox, a Scot, was lead singer for the Eurythmics, whose hits included "Sweet Dreams Are Made of This." Six-foot-tall Jones gave up modeling to sing and act. Performance artist Anderson blended graphics, mime, film, and music.

Wynton and Branford Marsalis

Ellis Marsalis was one of New Orleans's best-known jazz pianists and teachers. His sons Wynton *(right)* and Branford *(far right)* studied music in school, then built their own careers. In the '80s, Wynton and Branford brought jazz to a new, younger audience.

Branford played saxophone in jazz groups and with rock musicians. Wynton, a trumpeter, had been a successful classical musician until he felt the pull of jazz—America's "classical" music. Wynton and Branford have argued about whether jazz should remain in its pure form or if it can influence other styles. But there is no argument that America loves their music.

Using Music to Feed the Hungry

When news coverage of the famine in Ethiopia was beamed around the world, concerned people looked for ways to help. Irish singer Bob Geldof of the group Boomtown Rats used music to ease the suffering.

In December 1984, he put together a group of 40 British musicians (including Paul McCartney, Sting, and members of U2), and cut a record under the name Band Aid. All of the proceeds went to famine relief. In the United States, singer and humanitarian Harry Belafonte spearheaded a similar effort. A group of outstanding performers (including Michael Jackson, Stevie Wonder, Bruce Springsteen, and others)

recorded "We Are the World" to benefit USA for Africa *(left)*. By July 1985, the groundwork was laid for a historic concert.

"Live Aid" was a huge benefit concert televised worldwide. Musicians in London and Philadelphia *(below)* performed for more than 16 hours and ultimately raised $120 million.

Live Aid, U.S.A.

How Many?

Thriller

Released in 1982, Michael Jackson's *Thriller (above)* became the best-selling album ever. It sold more than 45 million copies, which was more than any other record at that time. It was the first to top the U.S. charts for 37 weeks and won eight Grammy awards, more than any other album ever!

Rap Music

Rap hit it big in the '80s. Rap started out in the '70s when young men delivered spoken messages over dance music playing in New York's discos. Grandmaster Flash *(below)* and others used rap to talk about gritty urban conditions or to convey political messages.

Madonna: A Material Girl

Madonna Louise Veronica Ciccone *(right)* took the world by storm in 1983. The dancer-singer's in-your-face style and skimpy black clothing was controversial. But it also set fashion trends and helped sell records, and even got her a movie role in a comedy called *Desperately Seeking Susan.*

Not unlike the character in her 1985 hit single, "Material Girl," Madonna is a successful businesswoman in an industry dominated by men.

Moving into a New Millennium

An economic boom in the 1980s led to spending cuts in the '90s to pay off debts from bad business deals. People lost their jobs as companies "downsized," or cut their work force, to save money.

Downsizing led to a recession, or slower economy, as people spent less money. The economy cost George Bush his 1992 reelection chances, and Arkansas governor Bill Clinton won.

Many people praised Clinton's leadership when the economy improved. But in 1999, he became the century's only president to go through an **impeachment** trial. The Senate finally acquitted him of charges that he had lied about his behavior in office.

Desert Storm

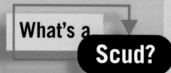

What's a Scud?

During Operation Desert Storm, Iraq used Soviet-made, ground-launched missiles called Scuds (below). Some landed without exploding. The Scuds were duds!

U.S.-led troops rescued Kuwait from Iraqi invaders in February 1991, protecting the Arab nation's oil fields from Saddam Hussein. Operation Desert Storm lasted for six weeks and left Iraq in ruins. About 200,000 Iraqi soldiers and civilians died; the United States lost fewer than 200 troops.

George Bush

President George Bush (above, with his dog, Millie) had an impressive career. A World War II fighter pilot for the navy, he received the Distinguished Flying Cross. He graduated from Yale University after the war, moved to Texas to start an oil company, and was a millionaire by the age of 41.

Bush was elected to Congress in 1966 and was U.S. ambassador to the United Nations from 1971 to 1972. In 1974, he went to China as U.S. envoy, returning to the United States in 1976 to lead the Central Intelligence Agency. He later served for eight years as Ronald Reagan's vice president.

As president, Bush won praise for his foreign policy, but a weak economy cost him the 1992 election.

Bill's Troubles

Throughout the course of his presidency, Bill Clinton was accused of lying about things he had done before and during his two terms in office. His wife, Hillary, claimed he was the target of a Republican-led conspiracy.

The couple's problems began when Congress hired Judge Kenneth Starr to investigate their role in a failed real estate deal during the '80s.

Starr hoped to show that Bill Clinton lied about many things in his life. When Clinton denied having a relationship with White House intern Monica Lewinsky, then later admitted it, Starr moved to have him impeached.

Some Americans wanted Clinton to resign. Others believed this was a private matter that should not involve the government.

George Mitchell's Peace

A retired U.S. senator from Maine was a key player in Northern Ireland's 1998 peace agreement.

Three years earlier, George Mitchell *(below, center)* had agreed to help with the peace talks. As a former Democratic majority leader, Mitchell was famous for his patience in the Senate.

Patience was needed to end almost 100 years of fighting between Northern Ireland's Catholics and Protestants. A locally elected assembly would now govern the country. Northern Ireland would remain part of Great Britain unless it voted to join the Republic of Ireland.

Home-Grown Terrorism

On April 19, 1995, hundreds of people were at work in Oklahoma City's Alfred P. Murrah Federal Building. Suddenly, a bomb ripped off the front of the nine-story building, killing 168 people and injuring many others.

At first, people thought foreign terrorists had planted the bomb. But two Americans were actually responsible.

Timothy McVeigh wanted to strike back at the U.S. government. He was angry when the government moved against a heavily armed religious cult in Waco, Texas. On April 19, 1993, federal officials had tried to break through the walls of the compound, when the buildings caught fire. Most of the cult members had died.

Because he helped McVeigh make the bombs, Terry Nichols was given a long prison term. McVeigh received the death sentence.

Positive People

Every **decade** has its share of heroes and heroines, and the century's last decade was no exception. Heroes have many qualities in common. One is doing what is right, even when it may be difficult or unpopular. Another is being persistent—working hard to get what you want.

Dr. Ben Carson, profiled at right, had to read two books a week as a child, then write reports on each—and this was not a school assignment! His mother made him do it to help him improve his grades. As a poor woman who could barely read herself, she knew the importance of a good education.

All the people on these pages have worked hard to be the best. Americans can be grateful for their contributions to our world.

Dr. Ben Carson

Ben Carson had to overcome many obstacles to become a world-renowned brain surgeon.

Raised by his mother in Detroit, Carson had a quick temper. When he almost wounded another boy in a knife fight, he decided to turn his life around.

Today, Dr. Carson is the chief of pediatric neurosurgery at one of the world's best hospitals, Johns Hopkins Hospital in Baltimore. In 1987, he led a team of 70 doctors in an operation that successfully separated twins who were joined at the back of the head. "Once I developed confidence in myself and began to believe that I was smart, then all of those innate abilities began to come out," he said later. "There's almost nothing you can't do."

What's a Nobel Prize?

Alfred Bernhard Nobel made a fortune inventing dynamite and other powerful explosives. But when he died in 1896, he left his money to reward those who helped the world in more peaceful ways.

His estate became the foundation for the Nobel Prizes, perhaps the world's most prestigious awards. Given yearly since 1901, the awards are presented for achievements in physics, chemistry, physiology or medicine, literature, and peace. In 1969, an award for economics was added.

Four institutions in Sweden and Norway review lists of nominees that are submitted by organizations around the world. Judges on six committees select the winners based on those "who shall have conferred the greatest benefit on mankind." Each winner receives a gold medal (above), a diploma, and a cash award.

Author Toni Morrison

In 1993, Toni Morrison became the first black woman to win a Nobel Prize. The American author was given the prize for literature because of her moving, magical use of language in such novels as *The Bluest Eye* and *Song of Solomon*.

Morrison—who is also a professor at Princeton University—is best known for writing about the lives of African Americans, and especially those of African-American women. In addition to the Nobel Prize, Morrison won the **Pulitzer Prize** for fiction in 1987 for *Beloved*, the story of an enslaved

woman who is haunted by the ghost of her daughter. Morrison loves writing, and says that working with words "is sublime."

John Glenn, Back into Orbit

Retired astronaut John Glenn made history again in 1998 when he became the oldest person to go into outer space. On October 29, the 77-year-old Glenn soared back into the heavens aboard a NASA shuttle. He participated in studies about the human aging process. He came back November 7, safe, sound, and every inch a hero, especially for older Americans. Glenn had been the first American to orbit earth in 1962 (page 73). He orbited the planet three times aboard *Friendship 7*. Shortly afterward, Glenn left NASA for a career in business and politics. He served as a Democratic senator for his home state of Ohio from 1974 to 1992.

Cal Ripken Jr.: The "Iron Man"

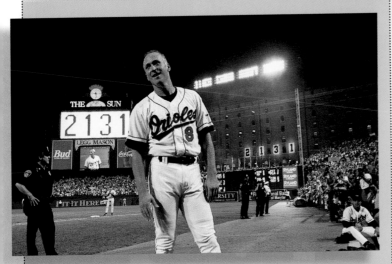

Baltimore Orioles shortstop Cal Ripken Jr. became a national hero just by showing up to work every day—for 13 years. On September 6, 1995, Ripken showed up for his 2,131st game in a row, breaking the 1939 record set by Lou Gehrig. As he told his fans, "Whether your name is Gehrig or Ripken, DiMaggio or Robinson, or that of some youngster who picks up his bat or puts on his glove, you are challenged by the game of baseball to do your very best day in and day out. And that's all I ever tried to do."

Famous 1 FIRSTS

Ben Nighthorse Campbell

Although Ben Nighthorse Campbell is not the first Native American elected to Congress, he is the first ever to chair the Senate Indian Affairs Committee. The Colorado Republican is one of the Senate's most interesting members. Son of a Northern Cheyenne Indian and a Portuguese **immigrant,** Campbell is a judo champion. In 1963, he won a gold medal at the Pan American Games, and he was the captain of the U.S. judo team that competed in the 1964 Olympics. Most Congressmen are lawyers, but Campbell is a jewelry designer, rancher, and trainer of champion American quarter horses. First elected in 1992, Campbell began serving his second Senate term in 1999.

Carol Mosley-Braun

In 1992, Carol Mosley-Braun became the first black woman ever elected to the U.S. Senate. The Chicago Democrat beat her opponent by winning 53 percent of the vote to his 43 percent.

Mosley-Braun has spent her career in public service. In 1973, a year after she finished law school, she became an assistant U.S. attorney. Six years later, she served in the Illinois House of Representatives. In 1989, she was elected the Cook County Recorder of Deeds.

Senator Mosley-Braun has inspired a new generation of black women to seek high public office.

Too Much Information

The "information superhighway" of the 1990s blazed a trail through schools, libraries, homes, and offices. Entire books, magazines, and newspapers found a home on the Internet. New businesses were launched. Folks could shop from their desks with a credit card and the click of a mouse.

A highlight of the **decade** was the expansion of electronic mail, or e-mail. Whether the address was across town or overseas, computers could send or receive mail for the low price of a local phone call.

But e-mail also brought new problems. Users got "spammed," or bombarded with junk e-mail. And chatting with strangers could be as unsafe on a computer as it was on a city street. Smart families made sure that everyone used the Internet wisely and safely.

Telecommuting

The '90s brought lower prices for fax machines, personal computers, and photocopiers, making it possible for more people to work from home.

Instead of buying gas for their cars, workers bought equipment for home offices like the one shown at right. These new telecommuters sent their work to the main office over phone lines, avoiding highway traffic jams.

Affordable technology encouraged more people to start their own businesses. An answering machine or voice mailbox could replace a secretary. Computer software kept track of finances, and

Web pages were great ways to advertise. Best of all—home offices had no dress code!

Internet: Surfers Up!

The World Wide Web was developed in Switzerland in 1989. By the mid-'90s, it was the world's largest on-line library, with thousands of "storehouses" linked together like threads in a spider web.

The connections are hyperlinks, highlighted words that can be clicked on to provide related information. If you're reading about animals, clicking on the hyperlink "cheetah" can take you to a Web site or article about cheetahs.

As part of the Internet, the World Wide Web has a client-server format. A server is like an electronic librarian—a program that stores and finds information. The client program delivers the information to a browser—computer software that displays it for you to read.

What's the Web?

The Internet connects computers worldwide via a language called TCP/IP (Transmission Control Protocol/Internet Protocol). Invented in the late 1960s by university users, the Internet was intended to make defense-related research less dependent on a central computer.

In the late 1990s, the Internet had more than 30 million "Net surfers," and that number was expected to grow quickly in the coming years.

www.com

Gadgets for People on the Go

Beepers

A pager message goes first to a computer terminal, where it is encoded. The terminal then sends the message to transmitters that broadcast it as a radio signal. The pager beeps its owner when the message is received.

Personal Organizers

By the late '90s, personal organizers were all the rage. This pocket-size computer could call up addresses, phone numbers, a calendar, a calculator—it could even transfer documents or send a fax!

Cellular Phones

A cell phone transfers calls via radio waves. Its name comes from the telephone system's geographic regions, or cells.

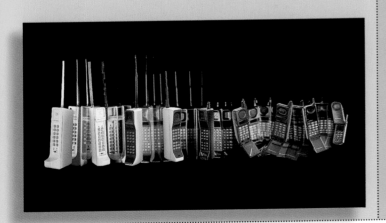

Martian Landing

A Robotic Explorer

On July 6, 1997, an 11.25-kg (25-lb.) robot named *Sojourner* *(above)* rolled out of the *Pathfinder* module and onto the dusty surface of Mars. Within minutes, it was testing soil and rocks, while *Pathfinder* recorded its progress.

What's in a Name?

Sojourner

NASA held a contest to name the robot explorer for Mars. Kids from around the world were asked to link the rover's mission to a worthy hero or heroine.

Valerie Ambroise, a 12-year-old from Connecticut *(right, bottom)*, came up with the winning name: "*Pathfinder* should be named Sojourner Truth because she is on a journey to find truths about Mars." In the 19th century, former slave Sojourner Truth *(right, top)* spoke out against slavery and supported women's rights.

Super Sports

Salaries for professional athletes soared in the 1990s, as TV networks paid billions of dollars to national professional leagues for the rights to broadcast games. In turn, advertisers paid dearly to show many more commercials during the games.

As networks paid team owners more money, players demanded their share. From August 1994 to March 1995, professional baseball players staged the longest strike in sports history. They protested an owner's ability to put a cap on their salaries.

Fans had little sympathy for their cause. A player's average salary was about one million dollars, whereas a typical family earned about $35,000 a year.

As game attendance dropped, fans voiced their anger. The national pastime had become just another business!

Michelle Kwan

Michelle Kwan's graceful moves on the ice won her a silver medal in the 1998 Winter Olympics in Nagano, Japan. The 17-year-old Chinese American wowed the audience with skill and style.

How 1 2 3 Many?

San Francisco 49ers star Jerry Rice is one of a kind! It's easier to ask what records he has not set than how many he has. The Mississippi native may be the greatest wide receiver in football history.

In 1994, Rice broke the previous record of 127 season touchdowns. A year later, he set a new record for rushing—with 1,848 yards. During the following season, he became the first player to snag 1,000 receptions and gain 16,000 yards. Rice was the first player to record four seasons of 100 catches each, and in 1997, he was the first nonkicker to score 100 points.

Airborne Athlete

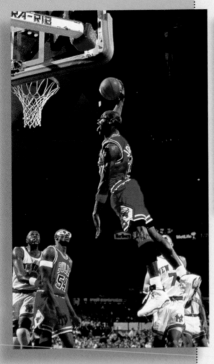

An American tourist at the Great Wall of China met a Chinese citizen who spoke little English. But the citizen grinned broadly at the tourist. "Ah, United States," he said, "Michael Jordan, Chicago Oxen!"

No other basketball star has this much worldwide fame. Jordan started wowing fans in 1981 as a freshman at the University of North Carolina at Chapel Hill. In 1984, he joined the Chicago Bulls, leading them to six NBA championships.

King of the Tennis Court

When a writer asked Pete Sampras how he'd like to be remembered, he said, "A nice guy playing good tennis."

In a sport known for big egos, Sampras stands out as a nice guy playing great tennis. In 1990, the 19-year-old was the youngest to win the U.S. Open. In 1998, he won his fifth Wimbledon title—the first American to win three years in a row.

A Great Tiger!

Eldrick "Tiger" Woods set new golfing records when he won the Masters Tournament in April 1997. At age 21, he was the youngest to claim the title, and the first Masters champion of African-American or Asian heritage.

Woods got his nickname from his father, Earl (below, right), who first gave the name to a young soldier he befriended in the Vietnam War. Tiger's mother, Kultida, is from Thailand.

Swinging into History

The entire world paid attention to baseball in 1998! Two talented players were closing in on Roger Maris's home run record of 61, unbroken since 1961.

All eyes were on Mark McGwire of the St. Louis Cardinals, a power-hitting first baseman nicknamed Big Mac. His challenger was Chicago Cubs outfielder Sammy Sosa.

The record fell on September 8 when McGwire whacked his 62nd home run. He hit eight more before the season ended, and Sosa swatted out 66!

Who would break the home run record: Mark McGwire (top) or Sammy Sosa (bottom)?

Trends at the End of the Century

There were lots of ways to spend **leisure** time in the 1990s—if you had the time! One could chat on-line at a cyber café, whiz around on in-line skates, tackle tough terrain on mountain bikes—the list was endless.

On the other hand, school seemed endless, too. To prepare kids for an increasingly competitive world, teachers, schools, and parents tried to strike the right balance between homework and extracurricular activities. Colleges and businesses wanted well-rounded students who played a sport or an instrument, took pictures—anything that showed dedication. Taking part in student government or community services could do the same. With such full schedules, kids could get a little stressed out. Nineties kids made sure that they took their fun seriously!

In-Line Skating

In the mid-'80s, in-line skating was something that ice hockey players and skiers did to practice during warm weather. Eventually, others discovered how much fun it was to swoosh around on one row of wheels instead of two. By 1997, more than 29 million Americans were in-line skating everywhere. About 40 percent of the skaters were 12 years old or younger, and 26 percent were teenagers.

Coffee Culture

Americans have always loved coffee, but in the '90s, almost everyone went coffee crazy. In the '60s and '70s, coffeehouses tended to be clustered near college campuses, but in the '90s they started springing up on main streets *(left)*, in malls, and inside bookstores. They served the basic American cup of java but also offered Italian coffee drinks such as espresso, cappuccino, and caffè latte. But perhaps the best thing about a coffeehouse was the welcoming atmosphere: a place where kids and adults could have a relaxing drink, enjoy a little conversation, or take time to read.

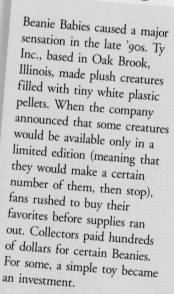

Let's **Compare**

Long Shorts

Five freshmen at the University of Michigan *(left, in blue)* changed basketball fashion in the early '90s with their long, baggy shorts. Before the "Fab Five," hemlines were high on the thigh. Ever since, most teams—from high school to the pros—have adopted the long, "jams"-style shorts.

Go Climb a Rock

Climbing rocks is not new. But climbing rocks indoors? Now that's new!

In the '90s, gyms and other athletic facilities installed walls so people could try their hand at rock climbing in safer surroundings *(left)*. Often textured like real rocks, the walls were equipped with hand- and footholds for climbers to grab.

Some people used indoor climbs to practice for an outdoor adventure. Sport climbing *(above)* with the proper safety equipment offered a physical challenge and a great view of serene natural surroundings.

Food

Wraps

Americans are always on the lookout for nifty ways to eat on the run, and wraps fit the bill. Chefs laid out oversize tortillas or Armenian flatbread; topped them with vegetables, spices, and dressing; added cheese, cooked chicken, or meat; and then rolled the whole thing up like a burrito. Sliced into bite-size circles or held in the hand, wraps were a big hit. Try one with your favorite ingredients!

The Top Toys

Beanie Babies caused a major sensation in the late '90s. Ty Inc., based in Oak Brook, Illinois, made plush creatures filled with tiny white plastic pellets. When the company announced that some creatures would be available only in a limited edition (meaning that they would make a certain number of them, then stop), fans rushed to buy their favorites before supplies ran out. Collectors paid hundreds of dollars for certain Beanies. For some, a simple toy became an investment.

Beanie Babies

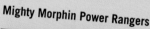

Virtual Pets

Microchips carried the programming for virtual pets such as the Giga-pet, Nano-puppy, or Tamagotchi *(above)* that would eat, sleep, and play only after careful— and constant— tending by their owners.

Mighty Morphin Power Rangers

On TV, the Mighty Morphin Power Rangers were teens who were given special powers to use against alien evildoers bent on world domination. Kids clamored for Power Ranger action figures to copy their heroes' martial arts moves.

Media Megahits

To revive was to thrive in the '90s. Movies took an idea from the past, added state-of-the-art technology, and a hit was born. Or reborn. Producer-director George Lucas rereleased the *Star Wars* trilogy with new scenes and special effects in 1997. Fans lined up, just as they had done two **decades** earlier. Fans also clamored to see the 1999 release of *Star Wars: Episode I—The Phantom Menace.*

Old TV shows got recycled as well. *Mission: Impossible, The Avengers,* and *Lost in Space* were remade for the big screen.

Radio stations cranked out disco and "classic rock" to appeal to nostalgic adults and their kids. Groups like Aerosmith developed a new generation of fans that knew Steven Tyler not only as a singer but also as the father of stunning young actress Liv Tyler.

What We Were Watching

The X-Files

The X-Files was a cop show with a twist: When FBI agents Fox Mulder and Dana Scully showed up on a case, the bad guy (or the victim) might just be an alien. Good plots and excellent special effects kept viewers entranced as they watched Mulder and Scully tangle with the **paranormal.** The show had a huge following at the end of the decade.

People — Spike Lee

Spike Lee has never been afraid of controversy in his quest to capture a realistic picture of what it's like to be an African American. Lee was born in Atlanta and grew up in Brooklyn. After attending Morehouse College, he studied film at New York University. His thesis was a movie, *Joe's Bed-Stuy Barbershop: We Cut Heads,* which won the students' Academy Award in 1982. His second film, *She's Gotta Have It,* won a prize at the prestigious Cannes Film Festival. Lee's films in the '90s included *Malcolm X, Clockers,* and *Girl 6.*

ER

Hospital dramas have been around almost as long as TV. One of the best was *ER.* Set in a Chicago emergency room, *ER* had a fast pace and sometimes quirky medical cases. Characters were complex rather than being all good or all bad.

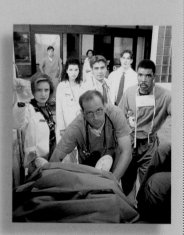

Dawson's Creek

Teenage viewers had a choice of several teen dramas, including *Dawson's Creek.* Each week, the gang from Capeside, Massachusetts, struggled to find solutions to the problems of growing up—crushes, school, and family troubles.

Fun Flicks

Toy Story

Ever wonder what toys do when nobody's around? The makers of *Toy Story* did, and their movie became an instant classic. The 1995 hit was the first full-length film to use three-dimensional (3-D) computer animation exclusively. Each of the 110,880 frames in *Toy Story* took an average of three hours to make.

Babe

In *Babe,* "a little pig goes a long way." So did the film; it won an Academy Award for best visual effects in 1995, and a Golden Globe for best comedy. The title character was actually a composite of 48 wiggly, pink Yorkshire piglets. To make it look like Babe was talking, the filmmakers used computer effects to blend images of a "talking" puppet pig snout with the rest of the pig's body.

What We Were Hearing

Selena

Before her tragic death in 1995, Selena Quintanilla-Perez introduced many Americans to Tejano, a form of music popular in south Texas. Her fans loved her down-to-earth style as well as her passionate singing.

Gloria

Gloria Estefan spent much of her early life nursing her father, who had multiple sclerosis. When she felt emotional, she'd go to her room and sing. Years later, the Cuban American was lead singer for the Miami Sound Machine, which played salsa-influenced music. Gloria's solo hits included "Can't Forget You" and "Don't Want to Lose You."

Latifah

Rapper Queen Latifah (born Dana Owens) brought a woman's perspective to a male-dominated musical genre. She staked her claim proudly with her first hit, "Ladies First." Latifah is an actress, too. She has made several films and starred on TV's *Living Single.*

Rolling Stones Gather No Moss

As the millennium neared, the Rolling Stones had been through it all—the death of a founding member, bouts with substance abuse, flashy romances and breakups.

Despite these problems—which might have done in lesser mortals—the Rolling Stones were still considered the world's greatest rock band.

Mick Jagger and his mates Keith Richards, Ron Wood, and Charlie Watts were part of the British Invasion of the '60s. Some 30 years later, in 1999, rock's bad boys toured, and Jagger, the world's fittest 56-year-old, strutted his stuff as though time was indeed on his side.

Hanson

The sight of Zac, Isaac, and Taylor Hanson *(above, left to right)* made young girls squeal with joy. The three brothers from Tulsa, Oklahoma, say they learned about pop music from a Time-Life collection of '50s and '60s hits.

20th Century at a Glance

The 20th century was one of rapid change. The availability of electricity led to the spread of industry and technology. Faster communications allowed people to talk across continents and oceans and even outer space. Medical advances allowed people to live longer, healthier lives.

But the people of the world also struggled with some of humankind's oldest problems. Wars large and small caused millions of deaths. And racial, ethnic, and religious bigotry led to fearsome violence as well.

Through it all, however, a spirit of hope, creativity, and strength has provided for many moments of beauty, courage, and outright fun. The timeline on this page and the following seven pages provides a brief overview of world events for one fabulous century!

First Self-Made Millionairess

Orphaned at seven, married at 14, a mother at 17, and a widow at 20, this daughter of former slaves created a successful line of hair and beauty products while working 14 hours a day as a laundress. Her incredible success made Sarah Breedlove McWilliams Walker (left, at wheel) a role model for African Americans—and for entrepreneurs everywhere. As America's first self-made female millionaire, Walker advised, "Don't wait for the opportunities to come. Get up and make them!"

Madame C. J. Walker

Politics and Military	The early years of the 20th century saw war and revolution, as countries tested various systems of government, including monarchies, democracies, and dictatorships.
Business, Labor, and Economy	Goods and services more than doubled in the first two **decades** of the century. Powerful industrialists took most of the profits, leaving little for the workers.
Science and Technology	Adventurers journeyed to the North and South Poles and conquered the air with the first successful flight of a motorized heavier-than-air craft.
Arts and Entertainment	The beginning of the century marked the start of our fascination with the movies. By 1920, moviemaking had become a multimillion-dollar business.
Daily Life	As electricity became available in more homes, daily life changed dramatically. Helpful appliances meant less heavy work and more time for leisure.
In the News	Women in democratic countries pressed for the right to vote. American women achieved their goal in 1920.

1900—1910

1901 The Commonwealth of Australia is established

1901 Queen Victoria *(right)* dies

1909 The NAACP is organized

1903 Milton Hershey builds a chocolate factory in Pennsylvania

1907 Ringling Brothers buys the Barnum & Bailey Circus

1900 Kodak introduces the Brownie camera

1903 Marie Curie *(right)* is the first woman to win a Nobel Prize

1903 The Wright brothers are the first to fly a heavier-than-air craft

1900 Baseball's American League is founded

1902 Beatrix Potter publishes *The Tale of Peter Rabbit (left)*

1900 The first hamburger is served

1903 Crayola crayons *(right)* are introduced

1908 Paper cups make their first appearance

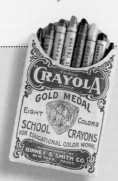

1901 The first Nobel Prizes are awarded

1910 Raymonde de Laroche *(left)* is the first woman to earn a pilot's license

1911—1920

1911 China's imperial dynasty falls

1914 World War I begins

1918 The Russian royal family *(left)* is murdered by Bolshevik revolutionaries

1918 World War I ends

1911 Chevrolet is founded

1912 The first self-service grocery store opens

1913 The 16th Amendment to the Constitution is adopted, establishing federal income tax

1911 Roald Amundsen is the first to reach the South Pole

1915 The first transcontinental phone call is made

1916 Albert Einstein *(right)* publishes his general theory of **relativity**

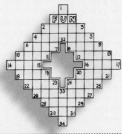

1911 The first Indianapolis 500 race is held

1913 The first crossword puzzle *(left)* appears in the New York *World*

1920 Baseball's Negro National League is formed

1914 Wrigley's introduces Doublemint gum *(right)*

1920 The first Miss America is crowned

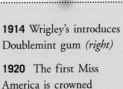

1912 Juliette Low founds the Girl Scouts

1914 The Panama Canal opens

1916 The National Park Service is established

20th Century at a Glance

1921—1930

Politics and Military

Europe and the United States exploited labor and natural resources in their colonies in Asia and Africa. World War II touched every continent on the globe.

1924 Native Americans are granted U.S. citizenship by an act of Congress

1925 Nellie Tayloe Ross becomes the first woman governor in the United States

Business, Labor, and Economy

Stock market failures in the major world capitals led to a worldwide economic depression.

1929 The U.S. stock market crashes

1930 The first stewardesses *(right)* fly for United Airlines

Science and Technology

The production and use of the atomic bomb cast a shadow over the future of the world greater than that caused by any other technological development of the century.

1922 British archaeologists uncover the tomb of the pharaoh Tutankhamen

Arts and Entertainment

Americans were listening to radio shows featuring music, drama, and comedy. Around the world there were eager audiences for books, paintings, and films.

1926 *Winnie-the-Pooh* is published

1929 Popeye *(above)* makes his debut

Daily Life

Passenger airlines, vast railroad networks, and widespread automobile ownership meant that more people were on the move.

1923 *Time* magazine *(left)* is founded

1926 The first electric pop-up toaster is available in the U.S.

In the News

Women grew more independent and adventurous. Historians and anthropologists were on the trail of ancient mysteries.

1926 New Yorker Gertrude Ederle *(right)* is the first woman to swim the English Channel

1927 Charles Lindbergh flies New York to Paris nonstop

1933 Adolf Hitler is sworn in as chancellor of Germany

1936 The Spanish Civil War begins; it will last three years

1936 Great Britain's King Edward VIII gives up his throne to marry a divorced American woman, Wallis Simpson

1938 Germany takes Austria

1939 German troops march into Poland

1939 World War II begins

1940 The German army enters Paris

1945 World War II ends

1947 India becomes an independent nation

1948 The Berlin airlift *(left)* begins

1949 The People's Republic of China is established

1931 Nearly 3,000 U.S. banks fail

1932 Unemployment strikes 12 million U.S. citizens

1933 Named Secretary of Labor, Frances Perkins is the first female member of a U.S. president's cabinet

1941 FDR outlaws discrimination in the defense industry

1943 Called the Big Inch, the world's longest oil pipeline to date runs from Texas to Pennsylvania

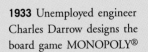

1933 U.S. inventor Edwin Armstrong devises FM radio

1935 The **Richter scale** is created to measure earthquakes' strength

1939 Kodak introduces the first color film

1941 The first aerosol can is patented

1941 English chemist John Rex Whinfield invents polyester fiber, later marketed as Dacron

1943 Jacques Cousteau *(right)* successfully tests his Aqua-Lung

1931 *The Story of Babar (left)* becomes an instant bestseller

1934 Donald Duck debuts

1934 Singer Ella Fitzgerald first perfoms at the Harlem Opera House

1941 The National Gallery of Art opens in Washington, D.C.

1943 The All-American Girls' Baseball League is formed

1947 *The Diary of Anne Frank (left)* is published

1933 Unemployed engineer Charles Darrow designs the board game MONOPOLY®

1935 The world's first parking meters are installed in Oklahoma

1935 London publisher Allen Lane launches Penguin Books, the first paperback editions of high-quality books

1937 The grocery cart is invented

1942 Wartime rationing *(right)* begins

1949 Timex introduces dependable, low-cost wrist watches

1932 Arkansan Hattie Caraway becomes the first female U.S. senator

1940 Four schoolboys discover prehistoric cave paintings *(left)* in Lascaux, France

1946 The first meeting of the United Nations General Assembly

1947 The Dead Sea Scrolls *(left)* are found

1950 The first transatlantic jet flight takes place

20th Century at a Glance

Politics and Military

The postwar period was marked by numerous independence movements in Africa and Asia, and by increased tensions between the **Cold War** superpowers.

1953 Queen Elizabeth II is crowned *(right)*

1955 The arrest of Rosa Parks *(below)* prompts a bus **boycott**

Business, Labor, and Economy

Industrial plants provided jobs and increased wealth for many. The unpleasant result was more pollution and wasted natural resources.

1957 The first commercial nuclear power plant opens

1959 The first Xerox commercial copier is manufactured

Science and Technology

Technological advances—some developed for wartime and defense needs—were made at a furious pace.

1952 The pocket-size transistor radio debuts

1954 The USS *Nautilus (right),* the first nuclear sub, is launched

Arts and Entertainment

America loved Broadway musicals and spectacular movies. Architects worldwide embraced the sleek, modern international style and designed buildings made of steel and glass.

1951 The first color broadcast of a Major League Baseball game

1955 Disneyland opens in California

1957 *The Cat in the Hat* is published

Daily Life

From television to toys, people had a wide range of choices for how they could spend their **leisure** time.

1951 U.S. direct-dial long-distance telephone service begins

1952 The first consumer microwave oven is available for $1,295

1954 Plastic contact lenses are developed

1956 Disposable diapers first appear on the market

1960 Felt-tip pens go on sale

In the News

Satellite technology allowed nearly instant communications around the world. Immediate coverage of breaking stories was provided by news organizations.

1953 Tenzing and Hillary *(left)* make the first successful ascent of Mount Everest

1959 The St. Lawrence Seaway opens, linking the Great Lakes and the Atlantic Ocean

1961 The Berlin Wall is erected between West Germany and **Communist** East Germany

1968 The Soviets invade Czechoslovakia

1968 At the Democratic National Convention in Chicago 10,000 anti-Vietnam War protesters demonstrate

1962 The first Wal-Mart opens *(above, right)*

1966 The MasterCharge credit card debuts

1969 Chemical Bank of New York opens the first automated teller machine (ATM)

1970 Amtrak is founded

1962 AT&T launches Telstar I, the first satellite to transmit TV and telephone signals from space

1963 Soviet cosmonaut Valentina Tereshkova *(left)* becomes the first woman in space

1962 *Dr. No,* the first film featuring fictional British agent 007, James Bond, premieres

1962 "Fingertips," by 12-year-old sensation Stevie Wonder, tops the music charts

1963 Schwinn Bicycles brings out the Sting-Ray *(below)*

1970 Medicine bottles adopt child-safety caps

1964 The Rev. Dr. Martin Luther King Jr. is awarded the Nobel Peace Prize

1968 Helen Keller dies at age 87

1973 The first U.S. prisoners of war (POWs) return from North Vietnam

1978 President Jimmy Carter of the U.S. leads peace talks with President Anwar Sadat of Egypt and Prime Minister Menachem Begin of Israel

1979 The U.S. Treasury Department issues a new silver dollar honoring suffragist Susan B. Anthony *(above)*

1973 The London Stock Exchange admits women to the trading floor for the first time

1978 The Coca-Cola Company signs a deal to sell products in China

1974 The pocket calculator appears

1976 Air France begins regular service of the supersonic turbojet Concorde *(above)* between Paris and Rio de Janeiro

1980 The Mount St. Helens volcano erupts in Washington State

1971 Jazz musician Louis Armstrong dies

1978 "Garfield the Cat" makes its first appearance in the comics

1979 Hungarian professor Erno Rubik presents his cube *(right)*

1980 3M introduces Post-it® Notes

1972 Nike athletic shoes are first available to general consumers

1976 Call waiting becomes available for home phones

1980 In-line skates hit the U.S. market

1971 The Soviet Union legalizes long hair on men

1973 Painter Pablo Picasso dies at age 91

1974 Thirteen-year-old Abla Khair of Egypt sets records as the youngest ever to swim the English Channel

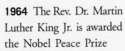

20th Century at a Glance

Politics and Military

The end of the **Cold War** eased tensions between the superpowers, but conflicts flared in Israel, Lebanon, Iraq, Yugoslavia, and Rwanda.

1981 Pope John Paul II is shot four times in an assassination attempt

1989 More than 500,000 Chinese students and pro-democracy activists lead a massive demonstration at Beijing's Tiananmen Square

1990 The Soviet Union breaks into independent republics after the end of **Communist** rule

Business, Labor, and Economy

Healthy economies were more dependent on service and technology jobs than on industrial production. Jobs and products crossed international borders.

1989 Time Inc. and Warner Communications Inc. merge to form the communications giant Time Warner Inc.

1990 The first McDonald's opens in Moscow

Science and Technology

The pace of discovery quickened. The Hubble Space Telescope provided new and startling views of our galaxy and beyond. The Internet radically changed how we communicate.

1982 Doctors at the University of Utah Medical Center perform the first transplantation of an artificial heart *(above)* into a human

1983 Apple Computer introduces the mouse

1984 More than 2,000 people in Bhopal, India, die from toxic gas leaked from a Union Carbide chemical plant

Arts and Entertainment

Computer-enhanced special effects and larger-than-life movie stars helped Hollywood's big action movies attract eager audiences around the world.

1982 Disney's EPCOT Center opens in Orlando, Florida

1984 The PG-13 movie rating is introduced

1986 *The Oprah Winfrey Show* first airs nationwide

Daily Life

In the United States, more than half of mothers worked outside the home. In spite of efforts to develop mass transit, the world's major cities were choked with commuter traffic.

1983 Compact discs (CDs) debut

1985 Nintendo Entertainment Systems become a hit

1986 Japanese cameramaker Fuji brings out the disposable camera

In the News

As the end of the century approached, natural disasters such as floods, famines, and earthquakes could not stop humankind's hope for a bright future.

1981 Britain's Prince Charles marries Lady Diana Spencer; 750 million worldwide watch the event on television

1984 South African bishop Desmond Tutu wins the Nobel Peace Prize

1991—2000

1994 Nelson Mandela is elected president in South Africa's first all-race election

1995 Israeli prime minister Yitzhak Rabin *(left, wearing tie)* is assassinated

1999 The North Atlantic Treaty Organization (NATO) mounts a military operation in Serbia

1992 Minnesota's Mall of America, the world's largest shopping mall, opens

1999 The Dow Jones **stock** indicator breaks 10,000; its highest point in 1991 was 3,301

1996 Scottish scientists led by Dr. Ian Wilmut clone a lamb from a cell of a fully grown sheep *(right)*

1997 The IBM supercomputer "Deep Blue" narrowly defeats the world chess champion Gary Kasparov in a six-game tournament

1993 Hong Kong action-movie director John Woo *(left)* directs *Hard Target,* his first film for U.S. audiences

1994 George Foreman beats Michael Moorer, almost 20 years younger, for the world heavyweight title

1990s Sport utility vehicles (SUVs) *(right)* top the U.S. market in sales, becoming many Americans' "car" of choice

1991 Theodor Geisel (also known as Dr. Seuss), author of *The Cat in the Hat,* dies at age 87

1999 Chicago Bulls megastar Michael Jordan retires from professional basketball

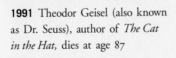

The New Face of South Africa

In 1991, African National Congress president Nelson Mandela began negotiations with South African president F. W. de Klerk to establish true democracy in South Africa. Mandela had recently been freed from a 27-year prison term for opposing apartheid, South Africa's brutal system of racial **segregation.** Finally, the system was dismantled. South Africa was transformed on April 27, 1994, as 16 million blacks stood in mile-long lines to cast their first votes. Mandela won the presidency by a landslide and established the nation's first multiracial cabinet.

Facts and Figures

Over the course of the 20th century, America added five states and saw its population more than triple. Better living conditions resulted in a 50 percent increase in the average life span for men and women. In the middle of the century, many Americans moved to big cities to take jobs in heavy industry. By century's end, only 25 percent of the country's population still lived in rural areas.

Immigration to the U.S.

1900–1940

- **85%** Europe
- **2%** Asia
- **less than 1%** Africa
- **3%** South America
- **9%** North America & Other

1961–1990

- **44%** Europe
- **17%** Asia
- **1%** Africa
- **30%** South America
- **7%** Other/North America

The data above were compiled by the U.S. Bureau of the Census. For the decades of 1941-1950 and 1951-1960, only white immigrants' country of origin was noted. Therefore, the data collected were not an accurate portrayal of immigration patterns for that period.

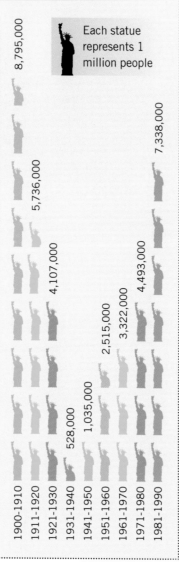

Each statue represents 1 million people

Decade	Number
1900-1910	8,795,000
1911-1920	5,736,000
1921-1930	4,107,000
1931-1940	528,000
1941-1950	1,035,000
1951-1960	2,515,000
1961-1970	3,322,000
1971-1980	4,493,000
1981-1990	7,338,000

Educational Trends

	Highest Grade Completed	Percentage of population
1901-1910	Grades 1-5	23.8
	High School	13.5
	College	2.7
1911-1920	Grades 1-5	22.0
	High School	16.4
	College	3.3
1921-1930	Grades 1-5	17.5
	High School	19.1
	College	3.9
1931-1940	Grades 1-5	13.7
	High School	24.5
	College	4.6
1941-1950	Grades 1-5	11.1
	High School	34.3
	College	6.2
1951-1960	Grades 1-5	8.3
	High School	41.1
	College	7.7
1961-1970	Grades 1-5	5.3
	High School	55.2
	College	11.0
1971-1980	Grades 1-5	3.4
	High School	68.6
	College	17.0
1981-1990	Grades 1-5	2.5
	High School	77.6
	College	21.3
1991-1996	Grades 1-5	1.8
	High School	81.8
	College	23.6

Domestic Consumption

Millions of Dollars

This chart shows, in millions of dollars, how much Americans have spent on various common items and services since 1930.

- ● Electricity
- ● Telephone
- ● Radios, TVs
- ● Books, Periodicals

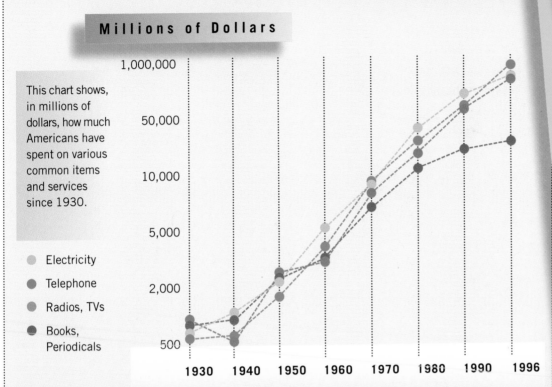

1,000,000

50,000

10,000

5,000

2,000

500

1930 1940 1950 1960 1970 1980 1990 1996

Try it!

Match the product to the year that it was introduced to the market.

1. Rollerblade
2. Paper clip
3. Skateboard
4. Electronic pocket calculator
5. Felt-tip pen
6. Velcro fastener
7. Popsicle
8. Hot dog
9. Lipstick

A. 1974
B. 1955
C. 1924
D. 1915
E. 1900
F. 1958
G. 1960
H. 1980
I. 1900

Answers:
1H (1980), 2E (1900), 3F (1958), 4A (1974), 5G (1960), 6B (1955), 7C (1924), 8I (1900), 9D (1915).

Changes in Costs

KEY
- Loaf of Bread
- Quart of Milk
- Toothpaste
- Dozen Eggs

$2

$1.50

$1

$.50

0

Year	1900-1910	1911-1920	1921-1930	1931-1940	1941-1950	1951-1960	1961-1970	1971-1980	1981-1990	1991-1999
Teachers' median annual income*	$328	$492	$970	$1,455	$2,794	$4,762	$8,299	$15,438	$31,400	$38,600

New Words & Phrases

Phrase/Word	Year	Description
astronaut	1929	one who travels in, or trains to travel in, space
briefcase	1917	flat case for carrying papers or books
carpool	1942	group who travels to work or school together by car
comic book	1941	magazine containing a sequence of comic strips
freeway	1930	toll-free highway
gung-ho	1942	extremely enthusiastic; from the Chinese for "work together"
motel	1925	lodgings with rooms accessible from an outdoor parking area
nerd	1950	intelligent, nonsocial person
slam dunk	1972	forceful overhand basketball shot

*Median income means there are equal numbers of people earning more than and less than that figure.

Picture Credits

The sources for the illustrations in this book appear below. Credits from left to right are separated by semicolons, from top to bottom by dashes.

Cover: Book spine, Armed Forces Collections, National Museum of American History, Smithsonian Institution, Washington, D.C.; front, Index Stock Imagery; National Portrait Gallery, Smithsonian Institution, Washington, D.C.; © Jay Hirsch—art by Chris Hopkins (background art).

3: Henry Ford Museum & Greenfield Village. **4:** Michael Ochs Archives, Venice, Calif.—Philadelphia Museum of Art: Louise and Walter Arensberg Library—CORBIS/Bettmann; National Archives, neg. no. 179-WP-1563. **5:** © Van Bucher/Photo Researchers—Trizec Hahn—*Daily Bread* Magazine/Jess Dyrenforth. **6, 7:** Chicago Historical Society—Kansas State Historical Society, Topeka; CORBIS—Circus World Museum, Baraboo, Wisc.; Special Collections Division, University of Washington Libraries, neg. no. UW 2315. **8:** The Granger Collection, New York—CORBIS/Bettmann—Library of Congress, photo by Edwin Levick, neg. no. LC-USZ62-11202. **9:** Brown Brothers, Sterling, Pa.; Library of Congress, neg. no. LC-USZ62-048757—CORBIS/Bettmann (2). **10:** Baseball Hall of Fame Library, Cooperstown, N.Y.—CORBIS; courtesy Boy Scouts of America; Smithsonian Institution. **11:** Brown Brothers, Sterling, Pa.; Culver Pictures, N.Y.; Museum of Modern Art/Film Stills Archive—property of AT&T Archives, reprinted with permission of AT&T; photos by Barbara Preorro Galasso/George Eastman House, Rochester, N.Y. (2); Metropolitan Museum of Art, Alfred Stieglitz Collection, 1933 (33.43.39), photograph © 1989 Metropolitan Museum of Art. **12:** Library of Congress, neg. no. LC-USZ-262-12876—CORBIS/Bettmann (2); CORBIS; art by Jeff McKay. **13:** Henry Ford Museum & Greenfield Village; courtesy Ford Motor Co.—courtesy Harley-Davidson Motor Co.; U.S. Steel—CORBIS/Schenectady Museum of Electrical History Foundation. **14:** American Heritage Publishing Co.—private collection; CORBIS/Bettmann (3). **15:** CORBIS/Bettmann—Photolabs, Royal Observatory, Edinburgh—CORBIS/Layne Kennedy; CORBIS/Bettmann (2). **16:** Brown Brothers, Sterling, Pa.—CORBIS/Bettmann/Underwood & Underwood—CORBIS/Bettmann; Library of Congress, neg. no. LC-USZ62-23725. **17:** CORBIS/Bettmann (2)—Deans Foods Vegetable Co., courtesy "Frozen Food Age." **18:** CORBIS/Bettmann—CORBIS/Mariners' Museum; Hulton Getty/Liaison Agency; CORBIS/Bettmann. **19:** National Archives, neg. no. III-SC-94980; Armed Forces Collections, National Museum of American History, Smithsonian Institution, Washington, D.C.—© 1927 by *The New York Times*. Reprinted by permission; CORBIS/Bettmann. **20:** Philadelphia Museum of Art: Louise and Walter Arensberg Library; Culver Pictures, N.Y.—CORBIS—Culver Pictures, N.Y. **21:** Movie Still Archives, Harrison Nebr.; CORBIS/Underwood & Underwood—UCLA Special Collections Department, George P. Johnson Collection; Brown Brothers, Sterling, Pa.; property of the Eaton Collection of the Special Collections Library of the University of California, Riverside. **22, 23:** Art by Maria DiLeo; CORBIS/Bettmann; National Library of Medicine; City of Philadelphia, Department of Records, City Archives, RG 78 Photographic Collection, Public Works, neg. no. 9527—CORBIS/Bettmann; NASA, photo no. 74-H-1065; © Robert Frerck/Woodfin Camp and Associates—CORBIS/Bettmann. **24:** CORBIS/Bettmann (all except bottom left), bottom left, AP/Wide World Photos. **25:** AP/Wide World Photos—The Granger Collection, N.Y.; CORBIS/Bettmann. **26:** © Harold Lloyd Trust/Archive Photos—Culver Pictures, N.Y.; CORBIS/Hulton-Deutsch Collection; the Kobal Collection, N.Y. **27:** Brown Brothers, Sterling, Pa.; National Portrait Gallery, Smithsonian Institution, Washington, D.C.—Jack Bradley; CORBIS/Bettmann; CORBIS—Michael Ochs Archives, Venice, Calif. **28, 29:** CORBIS/Bettmann—Hulton Getty/Liaison Agency; Culver Pictures, N.Y.; CORBIS/Bettmann; Palomar Observatory, courtesy AIP Emilio Segre Visual Archives—courtesy 3M; Lowell Observatory Photograph. **30, 31:** CORBIS/Bettmann (6); Brown Brothers, Sterling, Pa.—Brown Brothers, Sterling, Pa.; Culver Pictures,

Inc.; CORBIS/Bettmann. **32:** AP/Wide World Photos—CORBIS/Bettmann; paper photographed by Mike Pattisall; Library of Congress, neg. no. LC-USZ62-14459-901002. **33:** Margaret Bourke-White—CORBIS/Bettmann; Margaret Bourke-White for *Life* Magazine. **34:** CORBIS/Bettmann—National Archives—Brown Brothers, Sterling, Pa. **35:** CORBIS/Bettmann—National Museum of American Art, Washington, D.C./Art Resource, N.Y. 1965.18.12 William Gropper—© Charles O'Rear/Westlight; AP/Wide World Photos; Library of Congress, neg. no. LC-USZ62-C4-4890. **36:** Culver Pictures, N.Y.—property of the Eaton Collection of the Special Collections Library of the University of California, Riverside—Culver Pictures, N.Y.; National Baseball Hall of Fame Library, Cooperstown, N.Y. **37:** © 1998 Turner/the Kobal Collection, N.Y.; © 1998 Smithsonian Institution, Washington, D.C.—Hershenson-Allen Archives, West Plains, Mo. (2); MONOPOLY®, the distinctive design of the game board, the four corner squares, MR. MONOPOLY, as well as each of the distinctive elements on the board, and the playing pieces are trademarks of Hasbro for its properly trading game and game equipment. © 1999 Hasbro. All rights reserved. Used with permission.—CORBIS/Bettmann—photos by Al Freni, courtesy Ione Wollenzein (2); DC Comics Inc., 1938, 1965. **38:** Library of Congress, neg. no. LC-USZC4-4856-901403—Archive Photos; © Mark Segal/Panoramic Images—Golden Gate Bridge Highway and Transportation District. **39:** © Alan Schein/Stock Market; CORBIS/Bettmann; Topham Picturepoint, Edenbridge, Kent, England—art by Lori Cohen. **40, 41:** Anthony Potter Collection/Archive Photos—Shades of L.A. Archives/Los Angeles Public Library; National Archives, neg. no. 080-G-16871, CORBIS/Bettmann (inset)—National Archives; Library of Congress, neg. no. LC-USF34-73354-D—U.S. Army History Museum of Hawaii—National Archives, neg. no. 080-G-413988. **42:** Library of Congress, neg. no. LC-USZC4-4731—National Archives, neg. no. 208-YE-07; National Archives, neg. no. III-SC-19933. **43:** CORBIS/Lake County Museum—National Archives, neg. no. 179-WP-1563; Franklin D. Roosevelt Library, Hyde Park, N.Y.; CORBIS/Bettmann—Wide World Photos; Minneapolis Public Library, Minneapolis Collection. **44, 45:** *Life* Magazine—A. Y. Owen (4); National Archives, neg. no. 208-N-43888, CORBIS/Bettmann (inset); National Archives, neg. no. 999-WC-1059—Hulton Getty/Liaison Agency, N.Y.—National Archives, neg. no. 208-N-43468. **46, 47:** CORBIS/Bettmann; Archive Photos/Lambert, CORBIS/Bettmann (inset)—Hagley Museum and Library, Wilmington, Del.—CORBIS/Bettmann; art by Maria DiLeo; Mary Evans Picture Library, London; Bruce L. Brandenburg—Gjon Mili—CORBIS/Bettmann—Silly Putty is a registered trademark of Binney & Smith, used with permission; CORBIS/Bettmann. **48:** Reprinted by permission of United Feature Syndicate, Inc.; © 1996 Kunio Owaki/Stock Market—National Park Service, Mount Rushmore National Memorial—CORBIS/Bettmann—© 1986 Kunio Owaki/Stock Market. **49:** Hy Peskin, *Life* Magazine © Time Inc.; Herbert Gehr, *Life* Magazine © Time Inc.—Culver Pictures, N.Y.—Hy Peskin, *Life* Magazine © Time Inc.; Poperfoto, Overstone, North Hamptonshire, England—*New York Daily News* Photo; Movie Still Archives, Harrison, Nebr. (2). **50:** © George Holton/Photo Researchers; Computer History Museum Center—© Photo Researchers; © Bill Ross/Westlight. **51:** AT&T Archives, N.Y.; courtesy Polaroid Corporate Archives; U.S. Air Force Photo—National Archives, neg. no. 208-YE-22—CNRI/Science Photo Library/Science Source/Photo Researchers; Microfield Scientific Ltd./Science Photo Library/Photo Researchers; American Red Cross. **52, 53:** Courtesy Charles H. Jones, Reading, Pa. (inset), George Theofiles, *Miscellaneous Man*, New Freedom, Pa., photo by Neal A. Panzarella; CORBIS/Bettmann; Carl Iwasaki for *Life* Magazine; David Douglas Duncan—Michael Rougue—Robert Phillips/Black Star, N.Y.; art by Lori Cohen (2). **54:** Courtesy Hughes Electronics—New York Picture Collection; Sovfoto/Eastfoto. **55:** Courtesy March of Dimes—UNISYS Corp.; CORBIS/Steve Raymer. **56:** © Archive Photos, N.Y.—CORBIS/Bettmann; Everett Collection, N.Y. **57:** No credit—Photofest, N.Y.; CBS Photo Archive—Movie Still Archives, Harrison, Nebr.; CBS Photo

Archive—Ron Batzdorff/courtesy of Universal Studios and Imagine Entertainment. **58, 59:** Hirshhorn Museum and Sculpture Garden, Smithsonian Institution, Washington, D.C., Gift of Joseph H. Hirshhorn, 1972. Photographer Lee Stalsworth; Ralph Morse/*Life* Magazine; Joe Munroe—© Jay Hirsch; courtesy Campbell Soup Co., Camden, N.J.—© Van Bucher/Photo Researchers—courtesy Smithsonian/National Museum of American History, Smithsonian Institution, Washington, D.C.—© 1989 Mattel, Inc. All rights reserved. Used with permission. **60:** Hulton Getty Collection/Liaison Agency, N.Y.—CORBIS/Bettmann (2)—courtesy James Beck, A. J.'s Sport Stop, Vienna, Va. (2). **61:** Michael Ochs Archives, Venice, Calif.; courtesy Charlie Dick; Michael Ochs Archives, Venice, Calif.; CORBIS/Bettmann—CORBIS/Bettmann; Paul Schutzer, *Life* Magazine © Time Inc.; Photofest, N.Y. **62:** Wide World Photos/NGS Image Collection—Cecil W. Stoughton—courtesy the Peace Corps; paper photographed by Mike Pattisall. **63:** Larry Burrows; art by Alicia Freile—Walter Daran; Bernie Boston—AP/Wide World Photos. **64, 65:** Clayton Templin—Archives of Labor and Urban Affairs, Wayne State University; © 1998 Fred Ward/Black Star, N.Y.; CORBIS/Bettmann (2)—AP/Wide World Photos—© Jacques Lowe—Matt Herron; CORBIS/Bettmann (2); CORBIS/Bettmann. **66:** Robert Phillips/*Life* Magazine; Ivan Messar/Black Star, N.Y.—*Greensboro News & Record* and John G. Moebeb; Herb Orth. **67:** Charles Moore/Black Star, N.Y.—CORBIS/Bettmann; Associated Press Photo; Denver Public Library, Western History Dept. **68:** © Neil Leifer—the Kobal Collection, N.Y.; no credit; Walter Iooss Jr. **69:** © 1994 Joel Axelrod/Michael Ochs Archives, Venice, Calif.; Movie Still Archives, Harrison, Nebr.—Michael Ochs Archives, Venice, Calif. (3); Rick Friedman/Black Star/PNI. **70:** Archive Photos, N.Y.; John S. Clarke/Camera Press, London; Herb Orth. **71:** Saatchi Collection, London/Bridgemann Art Library, London; Archive Photos, N.Y.—Al Hartmann—© 1998 Charles Moore/Black Star, N.Y.; Alfred Eisenstaedt/*Life* Magazine. **72:** NASA, photo no. S69-31736—NASA, photo no. AS11-40-5875. **73:** NASA, photo no. S88-31387; Novosti, London; NASA, photo no. S66-36742—Ralph Morse/AP Wirephoto; art by Alicia Freile (2); the Kobal Collection, N.Y. **74:** George Tames/NYT Pictures; © 1974 Alex Webb/Magnum Photos, Inc.—Steve Northrup, *Time* Magazine © Time Inc. **75:** Courtesy Gerald R. Ford Library; Jimmy Carter Library—art by Alicia Freile—© 1998 Dennis Brack/Black Star, N.Y.; Alan Mingam/Liaison Agency, N.Y. **76:** CORBIS/Bettmann-Reuters; CORBIS/Bettmann—Carl Skalak Jr. **77:** David Rubinger, *Time* Magazine © Time Inc.—Harry Benson Ltd.—CORBIS/Bettmann. **78:** CORBIS/Bettmann—Greg Heisler, N.Y.; Ted Polumbaum for *Time* Magazine. **79:** © *Washington Post*, reprinted by permission of D.C. Public Library—Bettye Lane, N.Y.; J. P. Laffont/Sygma—CORBIS/Bettmann (2). **80:** Intel Corporation—© Jim Wilson/Woodfin Camp & Associates, N.Y. **81:** NASA, photo no. 71-H-709; Texas Instruments—Philips Electronics, North America—S.C. Delaney/EPA; no credit. **82:** Superman: The Movie © 1978 Film Export A.G. Superman is a registered trademark of DC Comics Inc.—© Randy Taylor/Sygma; Movie Still Archives, Harrison, Nebr. (2). **83:** The Kobal Collection, N.Y. (2); Trizec Hahn—Globe Photos, N.Y.; Steve Schapiro/Sygma—Movie Still Archives, Harrison, Nebr. **84:** © Michael Montfort/Michael Ochs Archives, Venice, Calif.—the Kobal Collection; Ted Soqui/Sygma. **85:** Michael Ochs Archives, Venice, Calif.—© 1991 Michael Montfort/Michael Ochs Archives, Venice, Calif.—Michael Ochs Archives/Venice, Calif.; © Barry Morgenstein/Retna Ltd., N.Y. **86:** © 1999 ABC, Inc.—Popular Culture Archives; courtesy Trustees of the V & A/photo by M. K. Egeli, London; photograph by Francesco Scavullo, © 1974, Newsweek, Inc. All rights reserved. Reprinted by permission. **87:** Mike Pattisall; Popular Culture Archives—Al Freni—Andrew Eccles/Rebus, Inc.; Mike Pattisall; courtesy Antonio Alcalá. **88:** Ronald Reagan Library, Simi Valley, Calif.—David Hume Kennerly; Terry Ashe. **89:** Ronald Reagan Library, Simi Valley, Calif.; Movie Still Archives, Harrison, Nebr.—Ira Wyman/Sygma, N.Y—CORBIS/Bettmann; John Chiasson/Liaison Agency, N.Y.; Bob Hallinen/Liaison Agen-

cy, N.Y. **90:** © Alex Quesada/Woodfin Camp & Associates, N.Y.; art by Will Nelson. **91:** Courtesy CNN, Atlanta, Ga.—MTV; © Larry Downing/Woodfin Camp & Associates, Inc.—CORBIS/Bettmann-UPI; AT&T Archives (2). **92:** Map by John Drummond—AP/Wide World Photos—NIBSC/Science Photo Library/Science Source/Photo Researchers; London School of Hygiene & Tropical Medicine/Science Photo Library/Science Source/Photo Researchers. **93:** Michele McDonald; NASA, photo no. S85-44253 (inset)—Amana Appliances; NASA, photo no. S84-37256. **94:** James Blair/NGS Image Collection—Mike Pattisall; art by Maria DiLeo (3); Photofest, N.Y. **95:** Globe Photos, N.Y.; © Thierry Martinez/Allsport USA—AP Photo/Elke Bruhn-Hoffmann. **96, 97:** © Waring Abbott/Michael Ochs Archives, Venice, Calif.—© David Corio/Retna Ltd., N.Y.—Michael Ochs Archives, Venice, Calif.; Sygma, N.Y.; Benson/Gamma Liaison Network Ltd.—© Anne Fishbein/Michael Ochs Archives, Venice, Calif.; Michael Ochs Archives, Venice, Calif.; Al Pereira/Star File, N.Y.; Globe Photos, N.Y. **98:** U.S. Air Force Photo; Noel Quidu/Gamma Liaison; Sygma, N.Y. **99:** Reuters/Gary Hershorn/Archives Photos—Agence France-Presse—© FEMA/Gamma Liaison—Gamma Liaison; AP/David Longstreath. **100:** Vince Rodriguez, Johns Hopkins Children's Center—R. Phillips/Image Bank; Rick Maiman/Sygma, N.Y. **101:** Ralph Morse, *Life* Magazine © Time Inc.; courtesy Ben Nighthorse Campbell—courtesy the Baltimore Orioles, Jerry Wachter Photography Ltd.; office of Carol Moseley Braun, U.S. House of Representatives. **102:** William Steele. **103:** Motorola—Sharp Electronics Corp.—Motorola; NASA, photo no. PIA01122—Detroit Public Library, Burton Historical Collection—Planetary Society/Jim Pickerall. **104:** © 1994 Stephen Dunn/Allsport USA; CORBIS/Jay Gorodetzer. **105:** Manny Millan/*Sports Illustrated*; © Russell/Liaison Agency, N.Y.—© George Lange/CORBIS Outline; John Biever/*Sports Illustrated*—Steven Green/*Sports Illustrated*. **106:** Jess Dyrenforth courtesy *Daily Bread* Magazine—Robert Moss Photography, Alexandria, Va. **107:** John W. McDonough/*Sports Illustrated*; Michael Kevin Daly/Stock Market; Robert Moss Photography, Alexandria, Va.—Mike Pattisall; Kimberly Butler; Fox Family Worldwide/SABAN Entertainment—Mike Pattisall. **108:** © Evan Agostini/Liaison Agency; CORBIS Outline—the Kobal Collection, N.Y.—the Everett Collection, Inc. **109:** The Kobal Collection, N.Y.—Movie Still Archives, Harrison, Nebr., photo by Jim Townley; Celene Reno/Sygma, N.Y.; © Gary Gershoff/Retna Ltd., USA; © Jay Blakesberg/Retna Ltd., USA—© REDFERNS, photo by Paul Bergen; © David Atlas/Retna Ltd., USA. **110:** Indiana Historical Society. **111:** CORBIS/Bettmann (2)—Hershey Foods Corp.—CORBIS/Bettmann; Brown Brothers, Sterling, Pa.—*The Tale of Peter Rabbit,* by Beatrix Potter. Copyright Frederick Warne & Co., 1902, 1987. Reproduced by kind permission of Frederick Warne & Co.; Crayola, Chevron, & Serpentine Designs are registered trademarks of Binney & Smith. Used with permission; from *What's Gnu? A History of the Crossword Puzzle,* by Michelle Arnot, published by Vintage Books, 1981; courtesy William Wrigley Jr. Company—CORBIS/Bettmann; National Park Service. **112:** Culver Pictures, N.Y.—Lee Boltin Photo Library; the Everett Collection, N.Y.—Time Inc.; Roger-Viollet, Paris. **113:** Jean-Loup Charmet, Paris—De Sazo/Science Source/Photo Researchers; CORBIS/Bettmann—the Cousteau Society, Paris—CORBIS/Bettmann—National Archives, neg. no. 171-pp-5a—Zev Rabuan, Jerusalem, Israel. **114:** CORBIS/Bettmann (3)—© Alfred Gregory, Royal Geographical Society, London. **115:** Courtesy Wal-Mart—courtesy the U.S. Mint—Novosti, London; CORBIS/Museum of Flight—Photofest, N.Y.; courtesy Funk & Junk at http://www.funkandjunk.com—art by Maria DiLeo—courtesy Schwinn Cycling & Fitness, Inc. **116:** Hank Morgan/Science Photo Library/Science Source/Photo Researchers; © Theo Westenberger/Liaison Agency—CORBIS/Leonard de Selva. **117:** CORBIS/Miki Kratsman—Murdo MacLeod/Spooner/Gamma Liaison—Studio Valletoux/N.P.A./Gamma Liaison—courtesy Land Rover North America, Inc.—from *Green Eggs and Ham,* by Dr. Seuss, Beginner Books, a Division of Random House, New York, 1960; REX USA. **118, 119:** Art by Lori Cohen.

Glossary of Terms

Alliance (uh-**ly**-ence) Nations that promise to join together to fight a common enemy.

Altitude (**al**-ti-tood) The distance of an object above the earth's surface.

Amphibious (am-**fib**-ee-yuhs) The ability to operate on land or water.

Anarchist (**an**-ar-kist) One who opposes any form of government control.

Antibiotic (an-ty-by-**ah**-tic) A medicine that kills harmful bacteria.

Aristocrats (uh-**riss**-tuh-krats) People in the top levels of society, often with wealth or respected family backgrounds.

Armada (ar-**mah**-dah) A group of naval vessels with a common military mission.

Aryan (**air**-ee-en) A term used by Adolf Hitler to describe the "master race" that he felt should rule the world—those of Germanic, non-Jewish heritage.

Assassin (uh-**sass**-in) One who kills for political or religious reasons.

Assembly line (us-**sem**-blee lyn) A manufacturing system that has each worker perform a single task on objects that move past on a conveyor belt.

Auxiliary (awk-**zill**-yer-ee) A group that is associated with, but not a member of, a parent organization.

Blitzkrieg (blitz-**kreeg**) The German term for "lightning war"; a swift military attack.

Boycott (**boy**-cot) A refusal to buy products from a business as a way of protesting its policies or practices.

Bread line (**bred** lyn) A line of people waiting for free food.

Bribe (**bryb**) To pay an official to break a rule or law.

Camphor (**kam**-for) A whitish substance with a strong odor, thought to prevent infection.

Citadel (**sih**-tuh-dell) A fortress or castle.

Cold War (**kold war**) A "war of words" between democratic nations (led by the United States) and Communist nations (led by the Soviet Union).

Communism, Communist (**kom**-yoo-nism, **kom**-yoo-nist) Control of goods and services by the central government, which then distributes them to its citizens.

Concentration camps (kon-sen-**tray**-shun kamps) German-run camps where Jews and other political enemies were held during World War II until they could be executed.

Constitutional amendment (kons-ti-**too**-shun-uhl uh-**mend**-ment) An addition to the U.S. Constitution that changes or clarifies its original meaning. It must be approved by a two-thirds majority vote in Congress and by two-thirds of the state governments.

Consumerism (kon-**soo**-mer-iz-im) Concern that goods or services are safe and effective.

Contagious (kon-**tay**-juss) The period of time when a person can infect another.

Cultural diversity (**cul**-tur-uhl dy-**ver**-sih-tee) A group whose members represent different races, national origins, and cultures.

Decade (**dek**-ayd) A period of 10 years.

Dirigible (der-**ij**-ih-buhl) A lighter-than-air craft with a rigid frame surrounded by a gas-filled balloon.

Documentary (dok-yoo-**men**-tair-ee) A true-to-life film or video that captures real conditions or events.

Documented (**dok**-yoo-men-ted) Wrote a report on actual events or real conditions.

"Duck-and-cover" drills (duk and **kov**-er drilz) A time for schoolchildren to practice finding shelter under desks in case of a nuclear attack.

Embassy (**em**-buh-see) The workplace and home of a foreign ambassador.

Emissions (ee-**mih**-shuns) Substances that are given off in smoke or exhaust.

Environment (en-**vye**-ruhn-ment) Surroundings that affect the growth and survival of any living thing.

Evacuated (ee-**vak**-yoo-ay-ted) The movement of people from a threatened area.

Exposure (eks-**poh**-zhur) A frame of film that has been exposed to light as the photographer takes a picture.

Famine (**fam**-in) Hunger and starvation caused by poor farming conditions.

Feminist (**fem**-in-ist) One who is a strong supporter of equal rights for women.

Franchise (**fran**-chyz) Permission given by a business to sell its product.

Geiger counter (**Gy**-gur **kown**-ter) An instrument that detects levels of radioactivity.

Generation (jen-er-**ay**-shun) All those born in roughly the same time period.

Genocide (**jen**-oh-syd) Killing all those belonging to a particular race, nationality, or ethnic group.

Harlem Renaissance (**har**-lem **ren**-uh-sahnz) A period of artistic activity in the African-American community of Harlem during the 1920s.

Hysteria (hiss-**tair**-ee-uh) Becoming so upset or excited that one loses control.

Ideology (eye-dee-**ahl**-uh-jee) An individual or group's set of beliefs.

Immigrants (**im**-mih-grentz) Those who arrive in a country with the plan to live there permanently.

Impeachment (im-**peech**-ment) A legislature's charges against a public official with the goal of removing that person from office.

Improvisations (im-prah-vih-**za**-shunz) Things made up on the spur of the moment.

Inflation (in-**flay**-shun) A rise in the price of goods.

Integrationist (in-tuh-**gray**-shun-ist) A person who wants different races to live and work together.

Internment (in-**turn**-ment) A government action that imprisons a group for political reasons.

Interpreter (in-**ter**-pruh-ter) A person who translates a foreign language.

Leisure (**lee**-zhur) Time free from regularly scheduled duties.

Lynching (**linch**-ing) A murder by hanging committed against racial minorities.

Merger (**mur**-jer) The joining of two companies into one.

Migrations (my-**gray**-shunz) Movements of people from one area of a country to another, often to find better living conditions.

Misconduct (miss-**kon**-dukt) Wrong or illegal behavior.

Monopoly (mon-**op**-uh-lee) A company that buys out other companies that compete with it; becoming the only business to provide a product or service.

Nationalism, nationalist (na-shun-uhl-iz-im, **na**-shun-uhl-ist) Putting the interests of one's own country or race first.

Nisei (**nee**-say) Persons born in the United States to parents of Japanese origin.

Nuclear war (**noo**-clee-er **war**) Using atomic bombs as a weapon in a war.

Paranormal (pair-uh-nor-muhl) Unusual or supernatural.

Penny arcade (**pen**-nee ar-**kade**) An entertainment center for young people with pinball, carnival games, toys, and candy.

Picket lines (**pik**-et lynz) Lines of protesters outside a business who try to stop customers or workers from going in because of unfair practices.

Plasma (**plaz**-muh) The liquid part of blood in which blood cells float.

Polio (**poh**-lee-oh) A viral infection that attacks the spinal cord, often causing paralysis.

Progressivism (pro-**gress**-iv-iz-im) Wanting a government or business to improve or reform.

Prohibition (pro-hib-**ih**-shun) Not allowing something to be sold or used.

Psychiatry (sy-**ky**-uh-tree) The study of emotional disorders.

Psychoanalysis (sy-koh-uh-**nal**-ih-sis) The study of the unconscious mind.

Pulitzer Prize (**pull**-it-zer pryz) Prizes given for writing and journalism established by the estate of publisher Joseph Pulitzer in 1911.

Quonset hut (**kwon**-set hut) A large metal structure, shaped like a half barrel, often used as a temporary office or living space.

Recruiting (ree-**kroo**-ting) Signing up people to serve in an organization or the military.

Refugees (**ref**-yoo-jeez) Those who flee to another country because of an invasion, acts of violence, or unfair treatment.

Regulations (reg-yoo-**lay**-shunz) Orders or laws.

Relativity (rel-uh-**tiv**-ih-tee) A theory by physicist Albert Einstein that space and time are part of the same "fabric," and that large objects, such as stars, curve space-time around them.

Relocation camps (ree-loh-**kay**-shun kamps) Temporary camps for those who have fled one country and are waiting for permission to move to another.

Resign (ree-**zyn**) To volunteer to leave a position in a company or organization.

Richter scale (**rik**-ter skayl) Named for its inventor, Charles Richter, a way to rank the strength of an earthquake on a scale of 0 to 9.

Risqué (riss-**kay**) Sexy dress or behavior.

Scandal (**skan**-duhl) A shameful action that shocks the public.

Segregate, segregation (**seg**-gruh-gayt, **seg**-gruh-gay-shun) Kept in a separate group because of race, class, or ethnic origin.

Shah (shah) The title given to kings of Iran (formerly Persia).

Sitcom (**sit**-kom) Shortened name for the type of TV show known as a situation comedy.

Sound barrier (sound **bair**-ee-er) The point just before an aircraft reaches the speed of sound.

Stock (stahk) Having one or more shares—or units of ownership—in a company.

Stratosphere (**strat**-oh-sfeer) Layer of atmosphere at 10 to 50 km (6 to 10 mi.) above the earth that has the ozone layer.

Supersonic (soo-per-**son**-ik) Traveling faster than the speed of sound.

Synthesizers (**sin**-thuh-sy-zerz) An electronic keyboard that creates sounds similar to those heard on real instruments.

Temperance (**tem**-per-ence) Against the sale and use of alcoholic beverages.

TNT (**tee en tee**) The common name for trinitrotoluene, a powerful explosive.

Transfusions (tranz-**fyoo**-zhuns) Transferring blood from one person or animal to another.

Unconstitutional (un-kons-tih-**too**-shun-uhl) A practice that violates the basic principles of a nation's constitution.

Unemployment (un-em-**ploy**-ment) Without a job.

Vaccine (**vak**-seen) Dead or weakened bacteria or viruses that are swallowed or injected to make a person immune to the disease that they cause.

Vaporized (**vay**-por-eyezd) A solid or liquid substance that has been changed into a gas.

Zeppelins (**zep**-puhl-inz) Large, lighter-than-air vehicles with gas-filled compartments and one or more non-gas-filled sections for passengers.

Index

Index

M

McCain, Franklin, *66;* quoted, 66
McCarthy, Joseph, *53*
McDonald's restaurants, *59*
McGwire, Mark, *105*
Machu Picchu (ruins), Peru, *23*
McKinley, William, *8*
McVeigh, Timothy, *99*
Madonna (dancer-singer), *97*
Magazine cover model, *86*
Maiman, Theodore, *54*
Malcolm X, *65*
Mandela, Nelson, *117*
Marchers for equal rights, *9, 64-65, 66, 67*
Marconi, Guglielmo, *10*
Mariner 9 space probe, *81*
Maris, Roger, 31, *105*
Mars: missions to, *81, 103*
Marsalis, Branford, *96*
Marsalis, Wynton, *96*
Marshall, Thurgood, *65*
Martial artist (Bruce Lee), *82*
Means, Russell, *78*
Meat-packing plants, *12*
Medals, *44;* Nobel Prize, *100*
Medicine and health, 14, 51, *92;* fitness craze, *87, 94;* flu epidemic, *22-23;* physicians, *51, 55, 100;* plague, 23; polio, 55; viruses, *92*
Mergers: corporate, *90*
Mexican Americans, *40, 64, 109;* TV portrayal, *83;* walkouts, *67*
Mickey Mouse Club, The (TV show), *57*
Microchips, *80*
Microwave ovens, *93*
Mighty Morphin Power Rangers (TV characters), *107*
Military: headquarters, *50.* *See also* Wars
Miller, Glenn, *49*
Miniskirts vs. midi and maxi, *70*
Miranda v. *Arizona* case, *63*
Mitchell, George, *99*
Mod clothing: 1960s, *70*
Models, *70, 86*
Model T Fords, 12, *13, 16, 17*
Monkeys: space, *54*
"Monkey" trial (1925), *25*
MONOPOLY® (board game), *37*

N

Monster movies, *37*
Moon: first men on, *72*
Morgan, J. P., *13*
Morrison, Toni, *100*
Morton, Jelly Roll, *20*
Mosley-Braun, Carol, *101*
Motley, Constance Baker, *65*
Motorcycles: Harley-Davidson, *13*
Motown Records, *69*
Mount Rushmore National Park Memorial, S.Dak., *48*
Movies, 10, *11,* 20, *21, 26, 37, 68, 82, 84;* Reagan as star, *89*
Ms. magazine, *79*
MTV (Music Television), *91*
Murphy, Audie, *44*
Music and musical performers, *20,* 26, *27, 34, 49,* 60, *61, 68, 69, 84-85, 96-97, 108, 109*

NAACP (National Association for the Advancement of Colored People): founder, *8;* medal recipient, *34*
Nader, Ralph, *71*
Nagasaki, Japan: bombing, *44-45*
Native Americans, *21, 35, 41, 78, 101*
Navajo Indians: code talkers, *41*
Negro leagues (baseball), *36*
Ness, Eliot, *24*
New Deal measures (1930s), *34-35*
New York, N.Y.: art show, 20; buildings, *11, 16, 39, 50;* NRA supporters, *34;* V-J Day, *45;* voting by women, *18;* Wall Street, *25;* World's Fair, *38;* Yankees players, *30-31, 49, 60*
Nickelodeons, *11*
Nixon, Richard M., *56, 74,* 77
Nobel Prizes, *100*
North, Oliver, *88*
Northern Ireland, 99
North Pole explorers, *15*
NRA (National Recovery Administration): support for, *34*
Nuclear power plant, *78*
Nude Descending a Staircase (Duchamp), *20*

O

Oakley, Annie, *6*
O'Connor, Sandra Day, *88*
Oil crisis (1973), *75*
Oil industry, 12
Oil spill: effects of, *89*
Oklahoma: bombing, *99;* dust storm, *32*
Oldenburg, Claes, *71;* art by, *71*
Olympic athletes, *21, 36, 61, 67, 104*
Owens, Jesse, *36*

P

Pagers, *103*
Palomar Observatory, Calif., *50*
Panama Canal: construction, *8*
Paris, France: flight to, *28-29;* liberation (August 1944), *45*
Parliament/Funkadelic (band), *85*
Pathfinder mission to Mars, *103*
Peace Corps, *62*
Peanuts (characters), *48*
Pearl Harbor, Hawaii: attack on, *40-41*
Peary, Robert, *15*
Penicillin: source of, *51*
Pentagon (building), Va., *50*
Perry Mason (TV show), *57*
Personal organizers, *103*
Pet Rocks, *87*
Photography, 10, *11;* instant, *51*
Picket lines: labor unions, *16*
Pinball machines, *37*
Plague, bubonic, *23*
Plastics, *14*
Pluto (planet): discoverer, *29*
Poitier, Sidney, *68*
Polaroid photography, *51*
Polio: braces, *55;* vaccination, *55*
Pollock, Jackson: art by, *58*
Pollution, *89;* from cars, *81*
Pop art: 1960s, *71*
Post, Wiley, *39*
Presley, Elvis, *61*
Prinze, Freddie, *83*
Prohibition, *24;* enforcement, *24*
Psychiatry: father of, *14*
Pulliam, Keshia Knight, *95*

Q

Quonset hut: postwar housing, *46*

R

Radio, 10, *27, 36;* CBs, 87
Railroad construction, *6-7*
Rap musicians, *97;* Latifah, *109*
Rat control, 23
Reagan, Nancy, *88*
Reagan, Ronald, 88, *89*
Reeve, Christopher, *82*
Refrigerators: earliest, *29*
Relativity theory, *14*
Rice, Jerry, *104*
Rickenbacker, Eddie, *19*
Ride, Sally, *93*
Riggs, Bobby, *79*
Ripken, Cal, Jr., *101*
Robinson, Jackie, *49*
Rock-and-roll musicians, *61,* 69, *84, 85, 96-97, 109*
Rock climbing, *107*
Rockefeller, John D., *12*
Rockne, Knute, *31*
Rolling Stones (rock band), *109*
Roosevelt, Eleanor, *34*
Roosevelt, Franklin Delano, 33, *34, 35, 38*
Roosevelt, Theodore, *9,* 10, *18;* memorial to, *48*
Roots (TV show), *83*
Rudolph, Wilma, *61*
Rushmore, Mount, S.Dak., *48*
Russia: missile crisis, *62;* space effort, *54, 73, 115*
Ruth, Babe, *30-31*

S

Sadat, Anwar, *77*
Sagan, Carl: quoted, *81*
Salk, Jonas, *55*
Salsa music and dancing, *84*
Sampras, Pete, *105*
San Francisco and area, Calif.: bridge, *38;* earthquake (1906), *9;* Silicon Valley, *map 92*

126

Time-Life Education, Inc. is a division of Time Life Inc.

TIME LIFE INC.

PRESIDENT and CEO: George Artandi
CHIEF OPERATING OFFICER: Mary Davis Holt

TIME-LIFE EDUCATION, INC.
PRESIDENT: Mary Davis Holt
MANAGING EDITOR: Mary J. Wright

Time-Life Student Library
20TH-CENTURY AMERICA

EDITOR: Myrna E. Traylor

Associate Editor/Research and Writing: Nikki Trahan
Series Picture Associate: Lisa Moss
Editorial Assistant: Maria Washington
Picture Coordinator: Daryl Beard

Designed by: Lori Cohen, 3r1 Group

Special Contributors: William Clark, Patricia Daniels, Mark A. Galan, Victoria Garrett Jones, Robin S.H.T. Reid (text); Charlotte Fullerton, Jocelyn Lindsay (research); Barbara Klein (index).
Senior Copy Editor: Judith Klein
Correspondents: Maria Vincenza Aloisi (Paris), Christine Hinze (London), Christina Lieberman (New York).

Vice President of Marketing and Publisher: Rosalyn Perkins
Vice President, Production: Patricia Pascale
Director of Publishing Technology: Betsi McGrath
Director of Photography and Research: John Conrad Weiser
Marketing Manager: Michelle Stegmaier
Production Manager: Carolyn Bounds
Director of Quality Assurance: James King
Chief Librarian: Louise D. Forstall
Direct Marketing Consultant: Barbara Erlandson

Consultants: *Russell L. Adams, Ph.D.,* is chairman of the Department of Afro-American Studies at Howard University. A political sociologist, he has written extensively in the fields of human relations and history. He has also served as a curriculum materials consultant to a variety of governmental agencies in the United States and abroad.

Robert L. Johnston, Ph.D., is an assistant professor of history and American studies at Yale University, where he also serves as Director of Undergraduate Studies for the History Department. In addition to co-editing anthologies on 20th-century rural political history and the American middle class, Johnston is working on a book manuscript entitled *The Radical Middle Class: Populist Democracy and the Question of Capitalism in Progressive Era Portland, Oregon.*

Library of Congress Cataloging–in-Publication Data

20th-century America.
           p. cm. – (Time-Life student library)
           Includes index.
           Summary: Provides an overview of the politics, business, scientific discoveries, arts, and lifestyles of the last century, decade by decade.
           ISBN 0-7835-1356-9
           1. United States—Civilization—20th-century Juvenile literature.
[1. United States—Civilization—20th-century.] I. Time-Life Books. II. Title: Twentieth century America. III. Series.
E169.1.A114 1999
973.91—-dc21   99-24896
                                                                         CIP

OTHER PUBLICATIONS

TIME-LIFE KIDS
Library of First Questions and
  Answers
A Child's First Library of Learning
I Love Math
Nature Company Discoveries
Understanding Science and Nature

HISTORY
Our American Century
World War II
What Life Was Like
The American Story
Voices of the Civil War
The American Indians
Lost Civilizations
Mysteries of the Unknown
Time Frame
The Civil War
Cultural Atlas

SCIENCE/NATURE
Voyage Through the Universe

DO IT YOURSELF
Total Golf
How to Fix It
The Time-Life Complete Gardener
Home Repair and Improvement
The Art of Woodworking

COOKING
Weight Watchers® Smart Choice
  Recipe Collection
Great Taste–Low Fat
Williams-Sonoma Kitchen Library

For information on and a full description of any of the Time-Life Books series listed above, please call 1-800-621-7026 or write:

Reader Information
Time-Life Customer Service
P.O. Box C-32068
Richmond, Virginia 23261-2068